NAVAJO

Susanne and Jake Page

Harry N. Abrams, Inc., Publishers

Editor: Robert Morton
Designer: Judith Hudson

Library of Congress Cataloging-in-Publication Data
Page, Susanne.
    Navajo / Susanne and Jake Page.
    p. cm.
    ISBN 0–8109–3679–8 (hardcover)
    1. Navajo Indians. 2. Navajo Indians—Pictorial works.
    I. Page, Jake. II. Title
    E99.N3P34 1995
    978.9'004972—dc20   95-5579

Printed and bound in Italy

Contents

Preface

In the vast landscape of Navajoland the present and the past are themselves an instant.

East of Chaco Canyon in New Mexico, where the most enigmatic ruins in North America lie brooding in the sun, there is an enormity of empty space – arid, even forbidding. This is Navajoland, part of Navajoland anyway, not even a very big part. It is, for all the world, like a solidified sea, waves having petrified somehow into flat-topped mesas and ledges that stretch away beyond seeing. The occasional outcrop is like some gigantic god's cairn, marking what? Here and there, little conical hills, one of them topped by a crouching, colorless pile of rock that looks like the caterpillar with his hookah on the mushroom in *Alice in Wonderland*. Once, long ago, the caterpillar was surely an imposing butte, before that an imposing mesa stretching its perfectly flat backbone across the land, and long before that a portion of an unimaginably vast sea floor.

You can read about such things, such processes, in textbooks, and they still seem surreal, beyond imagination. You can see them out on the land, as if caught in a stop-action photograph, and these forces still seem beyond imagination, at once too enormous and inexorable and wayward, too time consuming, and too prosaic. It is easier to imagine that something akin to a mind has been playing out here, giving this creation meaning.

Certainly, the people of Chaco gave this region meaning, though much of it is now lost. They built not just extraordinary stone dwellings and cere-monial places that seem more like religious resorts or retreats than actual towns, but long, dead-straight paths, or roads, stretching away across the horizon. And about the time these people abandoned their works some six hundred years ago, there was another presence in the region, groups of presumed wastrels who hunted, gathered, and farmed a little, and whom the Spanish would come to call the Apaches de Navahu. It is said that these people trekked down from Alaska, perhaps along the great cordillera of the Rocky Mountains, perhaps west of them, perhaps east. Nobody knows. As for the Navajos themselves, they know where they came from: an entirely different world. They, the Navajo, the Dineh, the People, emerged into this world north and east of Chaco, near the San Juan River in an area noted for a feature most of the world calls Gobernador Knob.

In this region of northwestern New Mexico, a place these late-arriving people still call Dinetah, they found promise, a future, and meaning in the land with its phantasmagoria of shapes, always new in the sudden changes of light. They found places to establish households – distant, remote, often hidden camps. In the parsimony of the land they found sufficient moisture under the sandy soil to grow patches of corn they had somehow learned about on the trek. Here, too, they found the footprints of their gods in the sandstone and lava, their commandments in the wind. Theirs would be a life of surprises.

A dirt track leads from the road that runs east of Chaco Canyon, snaking out across the land and disappearing in the ledges and mesas. But for the dirt track there are few other visible signs of human life. One is the silent parade of powerline stanchions stretching to the horizon like finely drawn tarot card versions of the kachina spirits of the Hopi who lived far to the west when the Dineh arrived here. Another sign of life – perhaps the only one – is a roadside sign saying in neat white capitals on a red background: *Morgan will no longer do minor repairs*.

My wife, Susanne, and I drove past that sign years ago on some errand or another, and we never pursued this funny little feature of the Navajo Nation. I have often since then thought about that sign, wondering if Morgan is related to one of the former Navajo tribal chairmen of that name, and wondering also just what kind of repairs Morgan *will* do. Presumably, something to do with pickup trucks.

What was it about doing minor repairs that bugged Morgan? How, I wonder, would someone needing *major* repairs reach Morgan's place somewhere out there beyond the local horizon, miles down that serpentine dirt track? What does Morgan's place look like, I wonder – a typical Navajo camp with an octagonal log hogan, maybe a hogan of cinder block, a shade house made of tree limbs and leaves, a sheep corral, a few other buildings perhaps – but with a modern auto-repair garage in the middle of it all?

Or maybe Morgan is a jeweler, a silversmith. Or a specialist medicine man. It remains, rather satisfyingly, a mystery.

Morgan is one of almost a quarter of a million Navajos who live in an area the size of West Virginia (or, put another way, all of New England less Maine) that stretches from this region of northwestern New Mexico across the top of Arizona almost to Flagstaff, with a small bulge up into Utah and with three smaller "island" reservations elsewhere in New Mexico. There is no way that looking at a map will convey the vastness and remoteness of this place. The Navajo and the Hopi – whose reservation is in the approximate middle of Navajoland – are among the few tribes of American Indians who still largely dwell in at least part of what they consider their ancestral lands. This is surely one of the reasons why the ways of the Navajos are considerably intact, largely evolving as they always have done. This is a vivacious culture that has aroused sufficient interest on the part of other Americans that, it has been estimated conservatively, a shelf of works describing Navajo culture would be fifty feet long.

That being the case – and as Morgan represents the more than ninety-nine percent of Navajos whom Susanne and I do not know – a question arises: why are we adding another book to the shelf? The reason, quite simply, is that some Navajos asked us to.

In the late 1960s, Susanne was given a magazine assignment that took her to Rough Rock, Arizona, where a milestone in Indian affairs had taken place – the opening of one of the first Indian-run schools for Indians in the country. This assignment led to her photographing and writing a book, *Song of the Earth Spirit*, about some Navajo families in that area. This, in turn, led to an invitation by the Hopi to produce a book about them, a task we began together in 1974, with the book, *Hopi*, appearing in 1982. Eventually, at a reception in one of the congressional office buildings on

Capitol Hill in Washington, D.C., held for the tribal chairmen of the Hopi and Navajo, Ivan Sydney and Petersen Zah, respectively, Chairman Sydney presented Chairman Zah with a copy of our Hopi book. Chairman Zah immediately went to a corner and looked through the book, evidently examining every photograph. Then he crossed the room to Susanne and said, "We want one of these, but bigger."

The format of a book is a matter left up to the publisher, but the impulse to do this book was stimulated in us by a few Navajo families who also concluded that such a book would be a good idea. The idea was a volume that provided vignettes in pictures and words of Navajo people the way they see themselves at a particular time in their, and our, history.

Over the years, we have made so many trips to Navajo (which is a place and a state of mind, hence this book's rather inclusive title) that we have lost count, many of them since we moved from Virginia to New Mexico in 1988. This book is a visible result of those experiences we have had, so freely shared by Navajo friends, and (we feel impelled to note) unfunded beyond a publisher's normal advance for such a work. Susanne has always preferred to approach such things with as few encumbrances and obligations as possible – whether it is obligations to anyone other than the subjects who come before her cameras, or preconceptions, either philosophic, artistic, or sociological, on anyone's part. It is this self-effacing attitude – almost unheard of among photographers in my experience – that has earned her the trust of so many Indian people in the last nearly three decades. At the risk of intruding where I should not, I feel comfortable as a former editor of *Smithsonian* and *Natural History* magazines in saying that Susanne uniquely practices the artlessness of seeing Indian people as they see themselves – and that artlessness is the highest photographic art. The people to be met herein are quite simply friends of ours who are also Navajo people engaged in their own versions of Navajo life, and the photographs are part of an attempt to reciprocate the friendship and love we enjoy in Navajoland and in our own home in the company of these people.

Nor does the text pretend to explain Navajo culture. Instead, it tries to portray as clearly and straightforwardly as possible what these same Navajo individuals have suggested in various ways is most important to them. As a result, much of the text is about Navajo history and ceremony, the two being inseparable. Much of it is based on personal experience – some of it very personal – and all of it quite selective in behalf of people's privacy. It has all been greatly enriched, at least in the writer's mind, by the written works of scholars such as Paul G. Zolbrod and Peter Iverson among a host of chroniclers both Navajo and Anglo.

We are both aware that this volume appears at a time when Indian people are quite rightly suggesting that they should be the chroniclers of their lives. To this we agree. But mindful of our original invitation, and its iterations since then, we hope chiefly that this volume will in some way prove to be a useful memoir for future generations of Navajo people and that, in our own society, it will call forth an even greater respect for the astonishing group of people of whom our friends herein are a part.

And we hope that whatever errors have crept in, they are lacking only those kind of repairs that Morgan will not do.

Origins

"This is what the old people usually say," said Mike Mitchell about the topic of history. "You can study a lot of things, but if you don't study right, it's all over."

He was sitting in the passenger seat of our rental car, bouncing across the rough, sandy tracks out in the desert east of Lukachukai and north of Chinle, in the arid and beautiful heart of the Navajo Nation, if this vast stretch of various landforms can be said to have a single heart. We were on something of a pilgrimage. Mike, a medicine man of the Navajo, a man who specializes in herbal healing, wanted to take my wife, Susanne, and me to a special place he had not evidently been before, a place where an important event in his tribe's history had taken place. "If we don't remember, if we let our religion go," he continued in a soft and relaxed voice, "it's the end of the world. One day it will come."

We had been out of the car several times in the white sunlight, while Mike marched here and there, elegantly bedecked in his turquoise bracelets and necklace, pointing out this and that plant, saying what its Navajo name was, what it was used for, asking Susanne to photograph it. Some were medicinal, some merely held a bit of momentary nutrition just under the bark for the wayfaring sojourner. Now, the herbal lesson done, we were headed up near Round Rock for a particular canyon where the red rocks rose up straight and precipitous out of a necklace of boulders and earthy detritus, a flat-topped butte where important things had once happened in the course of Navajo history.

"The white people," Mike went on, "they've lost their history, lost their religion. That's why they have Jesus. They had to put a man in there, one man."

Mike's elders had told him a story about this canyon, about how some Navajos had been attacked by Spaniards and had fled into the canyon. Surrounded and besieged they had climbed to the top of the butte, a place so steep that the Spanish had no idea how to follow them. So the Spanish simply camped out below, it is said, and waited while the band of Navajos up on top starved. As things were reaching their obvious and desperate end, the Navajos had a council and called on their leader to do something that he was most reluctant to do – use some special powers that Navajos do not much like to discuss or be thought to possess. So, however painful it was for him, the Navajo leader summoned up these special powers, took a bead on the Spanish leader, obvious from his armor and finery, and within a short time the Spaniard died. The soldiers left in horror and confusion and the Navajos were able to descend from their aerie and go on with their lives, though the leader who had had to use such awful powers continued to be most uncomfortable about it.

Petroglyphs, pecked or (as here, near Sweetwater, Arizona) painted on remote rock faces, bespeak the Old Ones, the earlier residents of the region called Anasazi.

Mike Mitchell, herbalist and teacher, points the way to a historic site (above) after showing the desert's many gifts east of Round Rock, New Mexico – big leaf sage and clay.

"I've always wondered how they got up there," Mike said and, well into his sixties (I guessed), began to scamper up the thirty-degree slope of eroded rock. Susanne, laden with cameras, marched along behind him and I wheezed upward, clutching at branches and feeling especially pale. Several times Mike paused to stare at the columnar rock wall above us, which reached more than two hundred feet into the painfully blue sky. Several times he changed his mind, going in one direction, then another. Then he announced that he had seen what must be the place. Some fifteen minutes later, we stood next to the vertical rock face, panting (all of us, I was happy to note), and above us was the first of a series of little round holes in the rock, handholds and footholds that led, so far as I could see, into what rock climbers call a chimney, and on up to the top.

"There. I knew it was here," said Mike, satisfied with the predictable truth of his world. "Want to go up?" The first handhold was above my reach, and between us we agreed it was enough to have found the means by which the ancient band of Navajos had engineered their escape. The historical event in question is not, so far as I know, in any book. It may well be that the names of the participants are forgotten. But the event lives, and it is this sort of event that is involved in the Navajo sense of "studying right," the sort of thing that the forgetting of can bring on the end of the world.

Later that afternoon, out on the scrub-covered arid lands west of the mountains again, we came upon a yellowish outcrop of flat rocks. Mike marched purposefully along with all the confidence of a commuter heading for the train station he has used for years. He stopped and pointed down at the rock. There was a pair of dark impressions in the sandstone, looking a bit as if a truck had spun its wheels in mud.

"Those are the footprints of the Holy People," he said.

History comes in three essential flavors. One is the kind of history practiced by specialists in the academy (and their amateur wannabees) and depends almost completely on the careful examination of written documents. Another is called prehistory – the realm of the archaeologist – and is based almost entirely on the recovery and interpretation of artifacts (and human and other biological remains). A third is based on stories passed on, usually orally, like recitations.

In the first two kinds of history, practitioners attempt to determine exactly what happened, and then see if meaning of some sort can be inferred from those events (along with others). The documentary historian's problem, among others, is that he or she almost certainly doesn't have all the documents, and that some documents can simply reflect the lies or misperceptions of those who wrote them. The archaeologist deals with material that cannot lie but, at the same time, cannot speak at all on its own. He or she has to find some reliable way to find out what an artifact array is, and then what it means. And of course, they don't have all the artifacts. And the real problem for both historian and archaeologist is that much of history no doubt takes place – and probably the most interesting parts of it – without leaving either document or artifact. But what we know of history and prehistory is constantly changing, based on new material, and also based on new ways of looking, new angles of vision, sometimes leading to new meaning.

The oral historian, the tribal storyteller, has none of these problems. Or usually not. For him or her, the meaning comes first: the story illuminates meaning and always has, even if it changes here and there over time in the telling, or even if it varies in some details from tradition to local tradition within the tribe.

It is no surprise that there are various versions of who the Navajo people are, where they came from, and what has been their lot.

The generally accepted scholarly view of Navajo origins is based for the most part on the fact that the Navajo language and that of the Apache are alike, and both are derived from that of the Athapaskans found in Canada and Alaska. (It is also generally believed that the Athapaskans were late arrivals in North America, reaching Alaska long after other Indian tribes had populated the hemisphere.) In any event, either because of some social or ecological problems in the northlands, or perhaps just because of population increase, some of these Athapaskan people began to expand steadily into new territory, maybe a thousand years ago, or maybe more. Archaeologists have yet to pin that down, and they are uncertain of the exact route. It stands to reason that these dispersing bands would have proceeded into territory that they were best equipped to handle – the arctic and subarctic habitat of the Rocky Mountains. It also stands to reason that they bumped into other, already established people here and there along the way. Just what they might have picked up from such cultures depends on which side of the mountains they would have occasionally spilled out on as they proceeded southwards. One guess is that they journeyed through lands on both sides of the mountains, each group learning somewhat different approaches to things. It seems, for example, that by the time the people who would come to be called Navajos arrived in the southwest, they relied a good deal on farming as well as hunting and gathering. On the other hand, those who would be called Apaches relied almost completely on hunting and gathering. Agriculture was little known among the people who inhabited the Great Basin, west of the mountains.

The Athapaskans had begun moving south as small bands of hunters, gatherers, and fishermen. They built conical dwellings, used sinew-backed bows and single-shafted arrows, made flat coiled baskets, and used dogs for hauling their worldly goods. Their religion was presumably centered on shamanistic healing. It is guessed that along the way they learned some of the arts of agriculture, and pottery, and maybe how to weave. Thus configured, they arrived in the region of the Anasazi.

Just when this happened is not known – informed estimates vary from about A.D. 1000 to about A.D. 1500. Most scholars seem to split the difference, suggesting a date around 1300, which is just about the time the Anasazi were packing up and leaving their great villages. Whether the new arrivals on the scene had anything to do with that mysterious departure is barely guessed at. Probably not: there have been many reasons adduced for this sudden departure, ranging from climatic change to internal social and religious imperatives, and any one of them, or a combination of them, would have been sufficient cause. And the Anasazi lands were already surrounded with plenty of troublemakers, it seems, before these northern bands arrived in the area.

Whatever happened, it seems certain that once the Anasazi moved on, the region was quickly populated with these Athapaskan bands. (Otherwise, it is reasoned, other established tribes would have moved in.) And by the time the Spanish arrived in the region in the late sixteenth century, the Pueblo people along the Rio Grande in New Mexico, and the Zunis, were all pretty much surrounded by Apachean people. Living for the most part in bands and typically made up of extended family groups, they may not have identified themselves in any tribal manner that we recognize today, but they spread out throughout much of the American southwest.

What we call Western Apaches lived in much of the eastern half of present-day Arizona, with Chiricahua Apaches in southeastern Arizona and Mexico. In fact, it was the Chiricahuas and Western Apaches who kept the Spanish at bay for centuries, preventing Mexican settlements from penetrating very far into Arizona. The Spanish did, of course, find a way north along the Rio Grande and founded Nueva Mexico, but supply lines to it were long and thin, and also subject to harassment by Mescalero Apaches, who controlled most of southern New Mexico east of the Rio Grande.

Meanwhile, Jicarillo Apaches dwelled in much of northeastern New Mexico, and other groups, such as those who would become known as Kiowa-Apaches, lived east of the Pueblo settlements, taking on much of the culture of the plains tribes like Kiowas and Comanches, roaming as far south as Texas and beyond. Never especially numerous people, the Apaches nevertheless filled the empty parts of the southwest with a presence that was potent far beyond their numbers.

Those Apacheans who would come to be called Navajos hunted and farmed a large area stretching from north of Santa Fe to present-day Grants, New Mexico, west to the edges of Black Mesa in Arizona (Hopi country), and north into what is today Utah and Colorado. There they farmed, planting maize, and traveled far afield to hunt and to gather plants and plant products. If they had ever been what could be called nomads, they were now semi-sedentary.

They traded meat, hides, and salt to the Pueblo peoples, and occasionally fought with them, typically, it seems, over the matter of captives. For example, the first Spanish encounter with these people occurred near Mount Taylor when Antonio de Espejo arrived there from the west in the 1580s. At first their relations were friendly enough, but the Navajos-to-be asked that some of their people (who had been captured by the Hopis and whom the Spanish had just taken from the Hopis) be turned loose. The Spanish refused and fighting broke out, setting a pattern that would persist long after the Spanish left the area. Intertribal hostilities were not uncommon, but usually occurred as local outbreaks during long periods of peace.

Indeed, Navajos were often found in league with Pueblo people in their attempts to throw off the Spanish yoke.

By the early 1600s, the Spanish presence reached north up the Rio Grande beyond Santa Fe. The Spaniards had heard, from members of the Jemez pueblo, of a group of people living between Jemez and the Utes called *Navaju*, which the Spanish understood to mean "great planted fields" or "fields in a wide arroyo." There is some doubt about this, nor is it necessarily true that modern Jemez translation is correct: *Navaju*, it has been offered, derives from a word for "fields" and another for "take from." The name, variously spelled, stuck, first as Apaches de Navaju.

There are many other names in use today or formerly among the neighbors of the Navajo. They suggest the ambivalence with which these people, like any group of people which is "not us," may be regarded. Various Apache groups have called them "people above" (evidently meaning to the north), "corn planters," and "White man's prisoner." The Taos Indians and a few others called them "heathens," while the Laguna term apparently derives from "my friend." The Pauite and Ute words refer to "cane knives" or "reed knives." One Hopi term (among several highly pejorative ones) means "one who has a prominent forehead," and for the Yavapai, west of Hopi, the Navajos are simply "tall Hopis."

The Navajos refer to themselves as the Dineh or Dine, meaning roughly "the People." And their views of these early events – of their prehistory – is different. For, of course, it is sacred history. It is a long story, full of details, surprises, humor, poignancy, terror, heroes, scoundrels, evil, and good – a story of people attempting to find and create a world of order and beauty where each person can live a long and full life in harmony with everything else in existence. One commentator has suggested that it demonstrates the important concept among Navajo that thinking, speech, and the planning they make possible are the most creative of acts. It demonstrates, also, a blunt-spoken and psychologically sophisticated concern with reconciling the age-old duality of the sexes – and of sex. It explains the existence in the world of evil as well as good and, reiterated again and again in ceremony after ceremony, it is a prescription for living in such a world. There are many versions, differing in details, sometimes quite important details (for example, how many worlds existed prior to this one), but the chief participants and main events are largely the same.

The Navajo language has been much studied by missionaries, linguists, and ethnographers and, beginning in the nineteenth century, was transcribed in varying orthographies. In due course some medicine men let their ceremonies be recorded in this way. The various healing ceremonies led and performed by medicine men recount in meticulous detail large portions of Navajo history – a retelling designed to put the world aright, as we will see later – and it is largely through this medium that what has always been an oral tradition has entered the world's literature both in English and in a written form of Navajo.

The Navajo language itself is a complicated one in which a variety of sounds occur that are utterly foreign to a native English speaker and speller. These do not translate easily into a standard alphabet of twenty-six letters, so linguists go to great ends to derive orthographic means of rendering them, leading to forbidding pages with Os with lines drawn through them in various directions, umlauts, and a variety of other symbols adhering like barnacles to familiar letters, along with a host of other typographic means which, I would guess, bring a smile to the face of a Navajo.

Pronunciation of Navajo is also a trap for the nonlinguist. Many nonspeakers have, with all good nature, tried to say something as straightforward as hello and found that, by virtue of a minor mispronunciation, they have said something quite different and usually scatological. This definitely brings smiles to Navajo faces. In any event, the Navajo language now exists in written form, with more and more of its old stories and current usage in book and pamphlet form. There are Christian hymnals with familiar hymns singable in Navajo, and there is even a book called *Navajo Made Easier*, which is one of the most optimistic book titles in the world.

What follows in this chapter is an attempt to introduce Navajo history in a necessarily foreshortened manner, to provide the basic and most common elements of this long and astoundingly rich story that is so important to the Navajo identity. It is, of course, an extremely dangerous task especially for an outsider, for one is operating with several levels of possible misunderstanding. In the first place, this is what Western Civilization thinks of as mythology – a somewhat deprecatory word that really means "someone else's religion." At another level, many people are more or less comfortable reading the mythology of the ancient Greeks, for example, seeing it as part of their own tradition, while comparable Native American stories are seen as something else altogether – unfamiliar, even a bit bizarre. Why North Americans, so proud of having established a "New" World, have been so slow to appreciate the rich tapestry of creation stories and heroes available in such tales as those of the Navajo has puzzled many. The account here is by no means designed to overcome that reluctance, but to provide an introduction to what is important to all Navajos. It is based on several different accounts, most notably a short version compiled by the Navajo Curriculum Center in Rough Rock, Arizona, called *Navajo History*, and a far more full translation, *Dine bahane: The Navajo Creation Story* by Paul G. Zolbrod, published in 1984 by the University of New Mexico Press, a highly readable book that manages to retain the flavor of the oral tradition from which it arose while providing the reader with the appeal of a novel. The quoted portions in the following version are from Zolbrod.

It begins in a small world bordered on all four sides by ocean. It is populated by insect people (twelve kinds of insects, which also include bats) who are able to act, in some ways, in the manner of the people of today. While there is a difference between day (white in the east, blue in the south, yellow in the west) and night (black in the north), there is no sun or moon in the hard shell of the sky. The insect people – also thought of as mist people and air-spirit people – set to arguing, chiefly over their own disruptive adulterous behavior, and are ejected, crawling around the sky's shell seeking an exit into another world.

This second world is populated chiefly by various blue bird people (swallows, jays, and so forth) but is otherwise much like the first world. The exiles ask to join up with bird people and are accepted, but promptly commit

Puzzlingly large figures adorn a rock face (above); others attest to a prehistoric skirmish.

adultery with some of their hosts and are, again, summarily thrown out. They are assisted by Nilch'i, the Wind, in finding passage to a third world, inhabited chiefly by yellow grasshopper people, and the same adulterous behavior leads to yet another expulsion. By the time of the exiles' arrival in the fourth world, they are chastened. Being treated generously by a race of people who live in square houses, they hold a council and resolve "to mend their ways and to do nothing unintelligent that would cause disorder."

In this world, they also soon encounter Talking God and a number of other Holy People, immortal spirit essences of the world, who perform an elaborate ceremony, putting two ears of corn, one yellow and one white, between two buckskins. The Wind blows on the corn and they are transformed into First Man and First Woman, the true original ancestors of the Navajos. It was the Wind that had given them life.

When this wind ceases to blow inside us, we become speechless. Then we die.
In the skin at the tips of our fingers we can see the trail of that life-giving wind.
Look carefully at your own fingertips.
There you will see where the wind blew when it created your most most ancient
ancestors out of two ears of corn, it is said.

First Man and First Woman have several sets of twins, learn to hunt well, to farm, and make useful implements out of pottery. The sets of twins marry into a group called the Mirage People (thus avoiding the problems with incest) and First Woman, wanting to make the husband-wife bond strong enough to last through life, creates the penis and clitoris, which would learn to "shout." Before long, Coyote (an immortal trickster and powerful troublemaker) gets into the act, blowing some of his whiskers onto these organs, making them so attractive that it is determined that everyone should cover themselves in the presence of others.

For eight years, all was well in the Fourth World. The people acted intelligently and didn't create any disorder. First Man taught the people the names of the four mountains in the distance – Sisnaajini in the east (Sierra Blanca in today's Fifth World); Tzoodzil in the south (Mount Taylor); Dook'o'osliid in the west (San Francisco Peaks); and Dibe nitsaa in the north (the La Plata Mountains). The names would be retained in the next world. First Man also taught the people about the ways of the gods, or Holy People, who could perform magic and travel swiftly on sunbeams. But then trouble broke out.

First Man and First Woman got into an argument. One day, after her husband had brought home a fine deer for dinner, First Woman thanked her vagina for the meal. First Man was miffed, and grew all the more so when First Woman explained that if it were not for the vagina, the men would never do any of the work. As the argument heated up, First Woman proclaimed that women could exist alone and had no real need for men. In due course, First Man stalked out in a rage and took all the men (and all the tools they had made) across the river, where they would live alone, free of women.

Both parties got along fine, each on their own side of the river, for a while. There was sufficient food to tide the women through the winter and the men successfully hunted. The women would occasionally come down to the river and taunt the men with lewd gestures and raunchy calls, to make sure that the men longed for them. By the second spring of this separation, the women began suffering for lack of food, while the men had plenty, and some women drowned trying to swim the river.

Meanwhile, sexual longing grew on both sides of the river. The women tried to satisfy themselves with long stones, quills, bones, even cacti. The men sought relief by using mud or deer livers. In the fourth year of this unharmonious situation, the Owl came and explained to the men that the women were in great trouble, starving, many of them losing their lives in the river. The Owl pointed out that without the women, men could not reproduce. It was possible that the entire world would come to an end – perhaps even the sky and everything so far created. First Man pondered this, then sent a messenger who brought the women to the river's edge. First Woman admitted that she could not live alone without a man, and First Man apologized, and the two groups were rejoined.

In the process, two maidens were taken by a monster that lived in the river, Big Water Creature. Two people, accompanied by two Holy People, went into the water to rescue them, and succeeded easily, but failed to notice that Coyote had trailed them down into the watery realm, where he stole two of Big Water Creature's children and snuck off.

The next day, the Fourth World began to come to an end. A great tide of water began to approach them from the four directions. Needing to escape, they asked the Squirrel for help and he planted some nuts that became fast-growing trees. But they didn't grow high enough. The Weasel planted seeds of other fast-growing trees, but these, too, didn't reach high enough. Then two mysterious men, one old and one young, appeared with a bag of sacred soil gathered from the four mountains that marked the edges of the world. Once this was spread on the ground with proper ceremony, a great reed grew with an opening on its eastern side. Into this the people went, and the reed grew, always above the raging waters. Eventually the people were able to climb out and into the Fifth World.

In the retelling today of these old stories, the experiences and lessons learned by the people in their journey through earlier worlds are crucial to their ability to live in harmony with themselves, other people they will encounter, and the new spiritual figures (as well as previous ones) that inhabit the present world – by most accounts, the Fifth. But when they emerged into the present world long ago, it was a very different place from today.

To begin with, this new world needed to be embellished. First Man and First Woman began by forming the sacred four mountains in the cardinal directions from material brought along from the four mountains of the previous world. And these were then adorned and populated with gods as follows:

East: white shell, white lightning, white corn, gray doves; Dawn Boy
South: turquoise, bluebirds, blue sky, blue mist (that brings gentle female rain); Turquoise Girl
West: abalone, yellow warblers, black clouds (that bring strong male rain); Abalone Shell Boy
North: obsidian, blackbirds, gray mist (female rain), darkness; Obsidian Girl

In addition, two "winds" that had provided guidance to the Holy People in the previous world also came to this one and, along with two others, were installed in the four cardinal directions. These four winds were, in fact, aspects of the universal Wind, which endowed all natural things in this present world with life, thought, movement, and the means of communicating.

A number of events then took place in rapid succession. Talking God taught them to construct the first hogan from three forked logs locked together at the top, with two other logs forming the entrance which was always to face the east, where all prayers and songs begin (see drawing). Lightning aided them in learning how to build a sweat bath by placing rocks heated in a fire into a low-ceilinged structure and pouring water on them to make hot steam. Then someone died, the body soon disappearing from sight. Two men went to look for it and peered down the hole into the world that they had recently left. There they saw the dead person sitting, and soon died themselves, which is why the Navajos to this day prefer not to look upon the dead or upon the ghosts of the dead.

First Man and First Woman determined that each passing day's white, blue, and yellow light that alternated with the dark of night was too feeble. They thought about it a long time, and talked about it for a long time, finally deciding to make a sun and a moon. They made a round dishlike object from rock crystal, surrounded with turquoise, red rain, and shimmering swirls: the sun. A smaller dishlike object made of mica and bordered with white shell became the moon, and both were placed in the sky. The price for having a sun and a moon was that every day someone would have to die, but in reward for hard work on the earth, everyone who dies will eventually be placed in the keeping of the sun and the moon.

In those days the world was smaller than now, and, in its first day, the sun traveled closer to the earth. It grew far too hot on earth, and the people prayed to the four winds that each might pull his mountain back away from the center of the world. After several days, the winds had made the world the right size. By then it was clear that the night sky was too dark, especially when the moon did not come. First Man and First Woman gathered up pieces of rock-mica and First Man worked out a design on the ground. He worked very slowly, starting by putting a piece of mica in the northern sky where it would not move, so that night travelers could get their bearings. Gradually he produced several constellations, including the great crystalline ribbon of the Milky Way, and named them. Then Coyote happened by and complained that he had not been consulted about the placement of the stars, and that it was proceeding too slowly. Impatient, he took the remaining pieces of mica and hurled them into the sky, where they lodged helter-skelter, a visible sign of the everlasting disorder that is caused by the impatient Coyote.

Even in this new world, however, which some call the Glittering World, echoes of the old world haunted the people. A number of women who had abused themselves with cacti and other objects when the men and women had lived separately began to give birth. In each case they bore monstrous offspring, which were abandoned in the hopes they would die. But they didn't. Instead, they grew up to be enemies and destroyers, lurking here and there, and giving the people reason to live every day in fear. There was Big Monster who lived on Mount Taylor, the Bird Monsters on Shiprock, the Monster That Kicked People Off the Cliff, the Monster That Killed with His Eyes, Horned Monster, and many, many others.

Before too long, the monsters had devoured everyone but First Man and First Woman and four other people. First Man hoped that the gods would help them, but First Woman doubted it, saying that they didn't yet know what pleased or displeased the gods. One morning, First Man noticed that a dark cloud covered the crest of the mountain called Gobernador Knob today. First Man decided to investigate, saying that he would protect himself by surrounding himself with songs. Just as he got to the peak, amid lightning, thunder, and driving rain, he heard an infant cry. Finding the spot despite the storms, he discovered a small piece of turquoise in the form of a female, which he took down the mountain to First Woman.

In an elaborate ceremony, the Holy People created a female baby from the turquoise figure, and this would become Changing Woman. When she came of age, reaching puberty, a ceremony was held so that she would be able to bear children. Called *kinaalda* to this day (and described in a later chapter), the ceremony was held on Gobernador Knob. The rite included the dressing of Changing Woman in white beads, having her run four times in the direction of the rising sun, and the singing by Talking God of twelve songs called hogan songs.

Sometime after the ceremony, Changing Woman grew lonely and wandered off. She lay down on a flat rock near a waterfall with her feet facing the east and felt the warmth of the sun come over her and fill her. In time, she gave birth to twin boys. They would come to be known as Monster Slayer and Child Born of Water. As the boys grew older, they were repeatedly challenged to races by Talking God. Encouraged by Nilch'i, the Wind, they eventually grew strong enough and fast enough to outrun the god (who was extremely pleased). Meanwhile, the twins wondered who their father was and continually asked their mother, Changing Woman, but she wouldn't tell them, only saying that he was dangerous.

The monsters were also still dangerous. One day a monster approached Changing Woman's house and demanded that she give him her sons to eat. She explained that she had no sons, that the tracks the monster saw on the ground were tracks she had made with her hand to pretend that there were people around and lessen her feelings of loneliness. The monster was satisfied and left. On another occasion, when the house was entirely surrounded by monsters, the Wind blew up a gale around it big enough to protect the people inside. Changing Woman feared greatly for her sons, but they continued to go out exploring during the day.

One day the sons came upon a column of smoke rising from a hole in the ground. Peering down, they discovered Spider Woman. Invited in, the boys were ashamed, because they could not explain exactly who they were, not knowing who their father was. Spider Woman told them that he was the sun, and lived far above in the sky, and that the way to his house was dangerous. To get there one had to pass through the rocks that crush travelers, reeds that cut them to pieces, cacti that tear them, and boiling sands that turn them to ashes. But, Spider Woman said, she would tell them how to make the journey and give them charms and protection that would see them through the ordeal. She would also teach them how to pass the tests that their father would subject them to, for he would not be happy to see them. After surviving the obstacles in their long journey, the twins reached the sun's house to find him out. They told the sun's wife that they had come to see their father. The sun's wife was angry that her husband had not been keeping his distance from other women, but she kept silent and agreed to hide the twins when the sun came home at the end of his day's labor. As he settled down, his wife revealed the two hiding boys and demanded, "Whose sons are these?"

Before the sun could answer, the twins explained that they had made a long journey to see their father. But the sun would not believe they were children of his until they passed several ordeals. He made them smoke tobacco that could kill, eat cornmeal that was poisoned, and endure a killingly hot sweat bath, as well as flinging them against a wall of sharp flints. Protected by Spider Woman's magic, they survived all this unharmed and the sun was convinced. He offered them their pick of corn and plants, wild animals, domesticated animals, precious jewels, but the twins told the sun about the monsters, saying that they would like all those gifts later, but now they needed weapons.

The sun was at first reluctant, because some of the monsters were also his offspring, but eventually he let the twins take two kinds of lightning, suited them in armor made of flint, and sent them back to the world on a stroke of lightning. Their first challenge was the Big Giant, who dwelled near Mount Taylor and was known to go to Hot Springs to drink from a great lake there. The twins laid in wait at the lake and in due course the Big Giant arrived and spotted them. They exchanged taunting insults with the vast monster, who then threw four lightning bolts in succession, but each one missed, thanks to the protection given the twins by Spider Woman, or, some say, thanks to the Wind. At that point, a brilliant bolt of lightning came out of the sky from where the sun's disk shone, stunning the Big Monster. Throwing their own bolts, the twins killed the giant. They severed the Big Monster's head and his blood gushed into the valley in a torrent, which the twins succeeded in stemming by cutting a line across the valley with a stone knife. The giant's blood congealed into a solid black mass, filling the valley below Mount Taylor, and can be seen there today as what the white man calls lava.

Thereafter, the older twin, called Monster Slayer, took on the task of killing the other monsters, often aided by his brother along with chipmunks, ground squirrels, and other animals. He slew the Horned Monster, the Bird Monsters, the Monster Who Kicks People Off the Cliff, and all the other especially dangerous ones. That task over, the twins came across another group of monsters living in a room below the ground. These were Hunger, Poverty, Sleep, Lice Man, and Old Age. The twins threatened to kill them, but each in turn persuaded the warriors to spare him. Hunger said he was necessary to keep people eating, planting, and hunting. Without him, Poverty argued, clothes and moccasins would not wear out, and people would not make new and better ones. Sleep claimed to be necessary when anyone is ill or tired. Everyone knows that lice get in people's hair if they do not stay clean, and Lice Man offered himself as a good reminder. And without him, reasoned Old Age, there would not be room for new people on the earth. So the twins spared all these monsters.

Then they traveled to the four sacred mountains, from which they could see that there were no more monsters to be slain. There was now order and harmony in the world. Later, the sun joined them to discuss the disposal of the monsters' corpses and it was agreed that they should all be buried under the blood of the Big Giant at Mount Taylor. Occasionally today, one may see a few bits and pieces protruding from the rocks – a claw or a finger that was chopped off – and imagine that they are fossils. The sun then left, taking his weapons and armor, and leaving word that he would like Changing Woman to meet him five days hence at Gobernador Knob.

On the appointed day, the sun came to Changing Woman and asked her to come with him to the west, where he would establish a home for her, so that they could be together at the end of his daily labors. But she would have nothing to do with him. He tried to persuade her: "What use is male without female? What use is female without male? What use are we two without one another?"

After a long silence, Changing Woman explained that she would want a beautiful house, "floating on the shimmering water," with gems and animals all around her. And when the sun asked why she made such demands, she said, "You are of the sky and I am of the earth. You are constant in your brightness, but I must change with the seasons." And she said, "Remember, as different as we are, you and I, we are of one spirit. As dissimilar as we are, you and I, we are of equal worth. As unlike as you and I are there must always be solidarity between the two of us. Unlike each other as you and I are, there can be no harmony in the universe as long as there is no harmony between us. If there is to be such harmony, my requests must matter to you."

So it was agreed, and Changing Woman went to live in the west beyond the farthest shore, joined each evening by the sun. The twins went to live where two rivers join in the valley of the San Juan. And after summer rain, when the mist clears, the bright colors of a rainbow shimmer in the moist light and the forms of the twins appear to this day.

Far to the west in those olden times Changing Woman soon found her days long and lonely, and she yearned for mortal company. So, by rubbing skin from her breast, her back, and under each arm, and with the help of Nilch'i, the Wind, Changing Woman created four clans of humans: the Kiiyaa'aanii (Towering House) clan, the Honaghaahnii (One Who Walks Around You) clan, the To Dich'ii'nii (Bitter Water) clan, and the Hashtl'ishnii (Mud) clan. These were the first clans of the Navajo people and they journeyed by magical means eastward to San Francisco Peaks, where they began to spread out over the land. Over the years they were joined by numerous other groups or clans – the Honeycombed Rock clan, the Rock Corner clan, the Yucca Strung Out In a Line clan, the Dark Streak of Wood clan, and clans named Water's Edge, Sage Brush Hill, Willow, Zuni, Red House, Where the Waters Join, and many others. Big Water clan was the last. After that, the Navajo people increased their numbers only from within. It is said that this all took place as long ago as seven generations of men who have lived to a ripe old age.

There is still a Ye'ii or God whose body encircles the four sacred mountains, and it is within this area that the Navajo people are safe and protected. It is also on the southern edge of this land near Mount Taylor, where the blood of Big Monster blackens the land, that Navajos first encountered the Spanish in 1582 and a new kind of history began.

So brief a recounting of so elaborate a tale or series of tales perforce leaves out many things, including the great number of variations. And, as noted earlier, it may leave one thinking that this creation story is a pleasant and imaginative legend – something comparable to the way one might look back from, say, an American college education, on the mythology of the Greeks. But this is not at all the way most Navajos consider their origin story. It is a presence in daily life, coloring and informing the world and the way a person acts.

Vincent Craig is a Navajo living in Window Rock, Arizona, capital of the Navajo Nation, trained as a law enforcement officer but best known as a cartoonist for the Navajo *Times* newspaper. He is the creator of Muttonman, a caped crusader (the cape is a Navajo rug) wearing moccasins and tube socks. He came to have special powers from eating a sheep that had drunk water from the uranium-contaminated Rio Puerco (the result of a 1979 uranium spill). His escapades include handling a reservation-wide rebellion by sheepdogs and saving Navajoland from the Fry bread Monster. On one occasion, Craig published a cartoon showing a Navajo family visiting the orangutans in the Rio Grande zoo in Albuquerque. The apes were busily picking lice from one another's heads, and the Navajo child says, "Mom, look, they're playing our game."

Before long Craig and the newspaper received an outraged letter from a well-meaning non-Navajo, calling the cartoon offensive. The newspaper wrote the letter-writer back, as follows:

According to a Navajo story, everything in the world had to come before the Creator and justify its existence. For instance, hunger said it had to exist so people would appreciate times of plenty. Way at the back of the crowd were the nits (lice). Finally, the head nit came forward and explained the reason for the existence of lice: "There's nothing worse than a bored Navajo. If they don't have something to while away the time, they get in trouble." In Navajo beliefs, insects play important, respected roles in life.

A major feature of any version of the Navajo story is the early association of the people with the Holy People, those indwelling essences of everything in nature – from nits to mountains. In the earlier times, it is said, the Holy People acted more intimately, more in the manner of human interaction, with the people (as did the various animals, such as Coyote and the others). The Holy People helped the Navajos learn a variety of things, helped First Man and First Woman create the features of the present world, and taught the people throughout their journeys the proper ceremonies for various situations.

Navajo ceremonial life is devoted chiefly to what Anglo culture might call healing, but not healing in any conventional sense of Western medicine. Navajo healing means putting the world right, putting the "patient's" environment and his relationship to it aright, and this requires intervening among the Holy People, the inner essences of the things in the world – be they "good," or "evil," or capable of both. For it is among these forces that one must learn to "walk in beauty" or be ill in one way or another.

"Walk in beauty" is a phrase one often hears among Navajos when speaking English or signing a letter to an Anglo. The phrase is an English distillate of a very complex idea that lies at the heart of the Navajo view of a proper life in the world, the Navajo goal. The phrase that sums up this goal is "*sa'ah naaghai bik'eh hozho,*" and non-Navajo linguists have written reams of prose trying to explain its essential meaning and its nuances. *Hozho* has been identified as the central idea in Navajo thinking – roughly beauty. But it means far more than a mere aesthetic: it means order, harmony, blessedness, pleasantness, everything that is good, not evil, everything that is favorable to mankind, the overall general ideal goal to which everyone and everything strives. (It has been pointed out that English, for example, has no word that reflects both moral and aesthetic excellence.)

To oversimplify, as one must, the first part of the phrase – *sa'ah naaghai* – suggests the ideal completion of the life cycle through death at a ripe old age (*sa'ah*) as part of the active continuing recurrence of this life cycle among people and all other things (naaghai). The rest of the phrase means, roughly, according to the dictates of (or the requirements of, or the desired goal of) *hozho*.

According to one version of the creation story, an inseparable pair of beings arose from the package of healing remedies that First Man carried in his medicine bundle. They were Sa'ah Naaghai (Long Life), who would be the primary *thought*, the thinking, of all the Holy People, and Bik'eh Hozho (Happiness), who would be their *speech*. In this way, thought is seen as the power of creation, and speech is the means to its active realization.

Not surprisingly, these two central concepts are embedded in other ways in Navajo philosophy – in the very wind and air. The centrality of wind in Navajo thought has been very beautifully explored in James K. Neely's monograph *The Holy Wind in Navajo Philosophy*, and his discussion informs the following.

Each person has a wind that exists within, which provides the means for breathing, moving, thinking, talking. This wind arrives upon conception, sent by the Holy People from the four directions, and it is at the same time both part of the universal Wind and also made up of elements of that Wind. Accounts vary as to how many elements are involved, but two key ones are sometimes called *sa'ah naaghai* and *bik'eh hozho*. One is thus born in the ideal Navajo state.

As an individual grows, other winds enter and add to the wind within, bringing in time the ability to stand erect, to talk, and so forth. This combined wind is seen as one's own Holy One, but at the same time part of the universal Wind at large. Since every natural thing has its own wind, an individual is thus connected to all natural things and all natural things are participants in what many other cultures prefer to call the supernatural. The wind standing within, which can be equated with one's self, is sacred.

During the creation of this world, the winds were installed in the four cardinal directions where they would, among other things, serve as the means by which the Holy People could communicate with others. Thus, other elements of the Wind are messenger winds, sometimes named Wind's Child or Little Wind. And these messengers bring guidance to people from the Holy People. Entering via the corner of the ear, they provide encouragement to think and act properly, and they issue warnings if the individual is getting off the path. They also report back to the Holy People. It is something like having a conscience that is also a direct telephone line to the gods.

There are also bad winds abroad in the world, and if one is not careful to keep one's own wind good and strong, these bad winds can enter, leading to fault: that is, wrong thinking, bad talk, recklessness, and other inappropriate behavior. Some of the evil winds are thought to be ghosts departed from those who died before their time. They may exist in the form of whirlwinds. Other evil winds may arise as a result of witchcraft. In any event, if one allows the good wind to weaken and begins to act in a faulty way, the messenger winds provide warning. But, eventually, if the warnings go unheeded, the Wind withdraws its guidance. The wind standing within then weakens further and is eventually taken away, resulting in death. The best way to avoid all this is to pray, to petition the Wind for assistance in strengthening one's own wind and restore well-being and proper thought and action. *Bik'eh hozho*.

In this way, the chants and songs of the medicine man during a ceremony and the personal prayers of any Navajo are the active effort to intercede with the holy essences of the world so as to make it right – to recreate *hozho* when something has set it awry.

The Land and the People

The watchful, serene, and honored faces
of matriarchy. Previous page: Billy Yellow, a
medicine man.

Previous pages: a man pays photographic homage to three sisters standing before Monument Valley's Three Sisters formation. Here, the faces of three elder women reflect a lifetime of hard work and pride in achievement.

Be it sheep intestines (previous pages) or fry bread, a string bean or coffee, nourishment and the life-giving role of the woman and the earth are one.

For each generation, everything is new, be
it a modern conveyance or a traditional hogan
(as on the previous pages). About half of
all Navajos (now 230,000 strong) are youths.

As with rural children anywhere, the land is etched permanently, even inescapably, into their personalities.

Where there isn't a hill, a clever sledder can hitch a ride from a horse. Right, a boy and his grandfather move across the desert floor near Setting Hen in Utah.

The Road to Hweeldi

From Baldy Hill, a boy sees a vast land stretching beyond his home village of Crystal, New Mexico – a landscape populated with stories of the recent and ancient past, and thus with meaning.

Within a century after the Spanish general Antonio de Espejo's unfortunate meeting with a band of Navajos near Mount Taylor, the province of Nueva Mexico had risen up in revolt. From Taos all along the northern part of the Rio Grande, at Zuni and even as far away as Hopi, the people rose up in a carefully orchestrated rebellion and drove the hated Spanish out. This was the Pueblo Rebellion of 1680, carefully planned by a man named Po'pay from an underground ceremonial chamber called a kiva in Taos. Runners were sent out across the land carrying knotted strings to other pueblos. Each day a knot was untied until the last, so that most (though not all) of the Pueblo people revolted on the same day, killing local Franciscans and then converging on Santa Fe, the provincial capital. After several days under siege, the Spanish broke through and headed south on a long journey of harassment, eventually fetching up in El Paso, where many of them festered in humiliation for more than a decade. Then, in the 1690s, the Spanish returned and reconquered the region by virtue of superior arms and organization. They consolidated their rule along the Rio Grande and to the west, halting only at the Hopi mesas when the Hopis descended on their own easternmost village, Awatovi (which was pro-Spanish), and demolished it.

The Pueblo Rebellion and particularly its aftermath had a profound effect on the Navajo people living on the fringes of the Spanish presence. At this time, the Navajos were not what could be called an organized political entity. Instead, they lived mostly in small bands, with allegiances to family and clan but no overall Navajo leader. Each band had its own war leader, ceremonial leaders, and peace leader – positions held at the discretion of the people they served.

Navajos were a fairly widely dispersed people. They already had a reputation as fierce raiders when the Pueblo Rebellion occurred, and along with other Apachean groups, the Navajos engaged in the rebellion and shared in the captives that resulted. It was the reconquest that had the most lasting effects, however. Even before the rebellion there had been some trading and cultural exchange between the northern pueblos and the Navajos. And from the Spanish they had obtained horses for transport and metal for various tools. But when the Spanish returned, various Pueblo people, including many from Jemez pueblo, simply abandoned their homes and went to live among the Navajos in the San Juan Valley, where they plotted a reexpulsion of the Spaniards. But within a generation, any such hopes had evaporated, and so they simply settled in with their Navajo hosts. At the same time, a number of Hopis from Awatovi, fleeing their attacking kinsmen, linked up with more western Navajo groups.

Under a rock overhang sits a fragment of an Anasazi kiva near Sweetwater.

Archaeologists opine that in the San Juan Valley (loosely, Dinetah), the pueblo refugees most likely remained quite settled; the Navajos farmed, but roamed widely on hunting expeditions. There is evidence that before long the refugees (or their descendants) and the Navajos had quite thoroughly intermarried, and many pueblo traditions caught on. Indeed, it has been said that the Dinetah was for a time the center of a cultural development unrivaled in any other Apachean group. This cultural revolution was largely unwitnessed by the outside world and is now known chiefly through archaeological evidence and, of course, oral tradition. Pottery unearthed there from this period shows the distinct polychromatic designs of the pueblo style – the imaginative geometry of black on white or black on orange.

In the canyons and tributaries of the San Juan River, small pueblos (pueblitos) become the settlement pattern of choice, providing a more centralized society than the earlier pattern of disparate bands of Athapaskan heritage. Single- and multiroom stone buildings became the norm, some with plazas, towers, and walls. Apparently many religious interests and practices of the pueblos took hold. Evidence of this dating to the period is found scratched into the natural rock surfaces of the area as images of kachinas (the masked dancers central to the pueblo religion) and the hump-backed flute player kokopelli, a ubiquitous fertility figure that goes back to Anasazi times. Nevertheless, in this mixing of architecture, crafts, and religion, the underground rooms called kivas that are typical of pueblo religious life, never caught on: the Navajo hogan remained the religious structure of choice. One can only imagine the imaginative (and perhaps at times uneasy) blending of shamanistic healing ceremonies and elaborate, village-wide rain dances that must have resulted, the latter being associated with a more strict and controlled social organization than Navajo bands had ever practiced. One can speculate that such matters as clan membership became more important than previously, and various puebloan taboos, such as that against eating fish, are known to have been adopted at this time. But, it is assumed, the Navajo language reigned supreme and the puebloan refugees learned it, rather than vice versa.

Scholars suggest that most traditional societies resist change, but clearly this was not the case with the Apaches du Navaju, nor is it the case with the Navajos of today. The willing adaptiveness, almost opportunism, of the Navajos has not been satisfactorily explained, but two factors are often mentioned as contributing. The Navajos did not have any centralized form of political or religious leadership and thus had a greater freedom to respond in various ways to new notions, or to a crisis. Also, their language is dominated by active verbs which, as anthropologist Gary Witherspoon has pointed out, reflects their view "that things are constantly undergoing processes of transformation . . . and that the essence of life and being is movement." In any event, since this period of cross-fertilization, Navajo culture has diverged from its Athapascan roots and become quite different from that of other Apachean groups.

During these years, the Spanish threat (and occasional military outbursts) became less of a problem for the people in Dinetah, but as warfare with the white man lapsed after 1716, a new threat emerged – the Utes of the north. The pueblitos were best suited to defend against Indian raids.

Meanwhile, the people of Dinetah had taken on from the Europeans cattle, sheep, and wool, possibly goats and the making of cheese, as well as cotton, and peaches, building a diversified economy well adapted to the region. (Livestock – and in particular sheep – began to take on a vitally important role in Navajo life and economy later in the eighteenth century.) But the strains from outside (chiefly pressure from Utes) led to internal strains and it appears that the puebloan element and the Apachean element clashed. One can imagine the intensity with which religious leaders discussed the loss of *hozho*, of harmony, and the ways of regaining it. Beginning in the mid-1700s, there was a revitalization of older traditions and ways – a major shamanistic feature, the Navajo Blessingway ceremony came into (or regained) prominence, for example – and many puebloan traits and concepts were done away with, such as stone houses and the decorated pottery. Kachina dancers lost whatever role they may have played.

One night Susanne and I sat in a hogan made of logs with an earthen floor a few miles outside Tsaile in the Chuska Mountains and listened to Will Tsosie, Jr., explain some of these things. (The hogan was, in fact, one of several that functions as a unique bed-and-breakfast, coupled with a tailor-made tour service that Tsosie operates when he is not operating the Chinle school system's two mainframe computers.) Tsosie told how he had returned to this camp from college and gone into his grandfather's hogan to tell him some things he had learned while he was away. His grandfather was seated at the west end of the hogan smoking a cigarette and he listened while Will explained that he now knew where the Navajos had come from. He described the southward migration of the Athapaskans, some of them fetching up in the Dinetah. But Will's grandfather shook his head and said, "No, No." The Navajo people came into being within the four sacred mountains, he insisted. And, Will told us, his grandfather was of course right. What we think of as Navajo came into being when the puebloan people – chiefly the Tewa-speaking people from Jemez – joined and intermarried with the people who were in the Dinetah. And out of this mixture came the Navajo people and their special culture.

Will told us that he was of the Coyote Pass clan, of which there are two branches. His branch, the Turquoise branch, traces itself matrilineally back directly to people from Jemez who migrated north into the Dinetah. The other branch traces itself back in the same manner and to the same point of origin, but circuitously – to those puebloans who left their homeland to sojourn among the Hopi, moving eastward again after the troubles at Awatovi.

In the period of cultural emergence, up to about the middle of the eighteenth century, the Spanish had sought to missionize the Navajos with no success. Then Hispanic ranches began to appear in areas closer to Navajo lands. They were at first welcome, the Navajos seeing the ranchers as offering possible help in their constant difficulties with the Utes. But frictions developed, predictably, and in 1773, the governor of New Mexico (which then comprised present-day New Mexico and Arizona) essentially encouraged a Ute war on the Navajos in which the People lost innumerable warriors, as well as women and children as captives. In 1774, the Navajos waged a retaliatory war on the settlers (who were virtually all what we now call Hispanic – people of Spanish and Mexican Indian derivation), driving them out of their eastern lands. Governor Juan Bautista de Anza of New Mexico signed a treaty with the Navajos in 1786 that held sway until the 1800s, when expansion by New Mexicans started another round of retaliation and raiding. Historians say that the Navajos' success in the mid-1770s against the Spanish-speaking New Mexicans, and the economic success of the pueblo-influenced Navajo lifestyle, as well as the rising economic use of livestock, consolidated all these influences into what we now perceive as Navajo culture. Territorial expansion soon followed – not back northward where the Utes now held sway but west and south of the old lands called the Dinetah. There was room where the southern Apaches had been driven farther south, and to the west where the Navajos moved into Paiute territory in Arizona, in some cases absorbing people from that tribe.

Raiding became more common in this period, intensified by a desire for livestock. Navajos raided and were raided by other tribes in return. This was further intensified with Mexican independence. The prairie commerce of the Santa Fe Trail was warily permitted by the recently installed Mexican government. This trade, however, provided New Mexicans with better arms and the Navajos became a target for those who supplied captives to the slave market. Uncounted hundreds of Navajos (and people from other tribes) were taken to become servants for the New Mexicans; some were shipped off to Mexico to work in the mines. Treaties would bring raiding to a halt locally and temporarily – the return of captives was a major Navajo preoccupation in these dealings – but there was no overall tribal government at the time. A treaty with one group of Navajos was never seen by other Navajos as binding – a pattern that would persist, eventually baffling the United States government, which took over in 1846.

Nor were the Navajos unified in their attitudes toward all this warfare. As early as 1818, a group of Navajos favoring peace with the Spanish-speaking settlers separated themselves from the rest, eventually settling in Canoncito to the south (where their reservation is today, about a half-hour drive from Albuquerque on Route 40). They were dubbed the Enemy Navajo by their

A modern petroglyph depicts goats, a Spanish introduction, near Monument Valley.

own people in those days. Many factors apparently influenced individual Navajos on the issue of fighting or not fighting the settlers: wealth or lack of it, propinquity to European settlements, perhaps even age. Certainly the very cost of military action took an economic toll and created strain among the People.

This uneasy and often violent coexistence continued with little noticeable change when Spain lost control of its North American colonies to the Mexican revolutionaries in the 1820s. It continued well after 1846, when, after the brief war between Mexico and the United States, vast portions of what is now the American Southwest, including California, were ceded to the United States in the Treaty of Guadalupe de Hildalgo. By the time American soldiers arrived in Santa Fe to take command of the large area called New Mexico, the Navajos had a reputation as dangerous, accomplished, and uncontrolled raiders. Indeed, in the intertribal warfare of the times – a phenomenon that can largely be seen as fomented by the Spanish (and then the Mexicans) on the principle of divide-and-conquer, not to mention the desire to obtain the resulting slaves – the Navajos certainly could hold their own. What was (and has been until recently) overlooked is that much of this reputation was earned in the defense of what Navajos believed to be their land, and in an effort to retrieve their people from slavery. But some of the raiding, too, was simply that – a kind of piracy. When the stars and stripes were raised over Santa Fe in 1846, with high hopes of bringing peace and economic growth to a vast countryside plagued with intertribal, and Indian-European conflict, the Dineh had every right to be suspicious.

One can only speculate about the Navajo attitude to this changing of the guard. Some Navajos (who were aware of the change) might have imagined that people who had just run off Navajo enemies would logically be friends. And there would be those who would be standoffish and those who would know perfectly well that none of this boded any good at all. They would all be both correct and wrong in some ways.

It is true that, when the United States became the hegemon in this land, many other Indian people – in particular the pueblo people of the northern New Mexican Rio Grande – were hoping that this new Great

White Hope would succeed in ridding their communities of Navajo raids, whatever the motivation for the attacks. For the Navajos, still organized in localized family groups of probably no more than a hundred, but who would get together for paramilitary purposes, were part of the day's culture of raid and counterraid. This happened to be part of the overall way of things at the time and there is no purpose in denying it.

At the time of the American takeover, there were also thousands of Navajos enslaved by New Mexicans as well as other Indian tribes, but it is also clear that there were slaves among the Navajos. On both sides, slaves were employed in menial, unattractive tasks and chores. It was not a period of time in the evolution of human cultures that makes an observer today of any stripe uniformly proud, but it may be even more prideful to wish away what seem to be the facts about the past. No one's ancestors can be held responsible for all of their descendants' definitions and moral perceptions. To remind people that the Navajo turned out to be pretty darned good at raiding and vengeance in those days does them no particular injustice or embarrassment.

A Navajo man told me that in the old days Navajos were raiders, and I wrote it down and it was published, with attribution. On seeing it in print, the Navajo man said, "Did I say that?" His apparent shock was tempered, I had the feeling, by a not altogether improper satisfaction. The Navajos were not, in those days, very many and they could have disappeared, through outright destruction as a people, or by absorption. Instead, they remained the Navajo and a lot of their survival had to do with a well-calculated aggressiveness. (I would be surprised if Changing Woman was not urging her descendants on at that time, as she had her twin sons in the days of the monsters.)

Today the Navajo people take pride, justifiably and uniformly, in their ability to adapt to changing circumstances while maintaining their bedrock inner core as a unique group of people with a singular approach to the world that is largely intact. It would be unreasonable to imagine that this capacity doesn't have something to do with the following: their understanding of human nature as revealed in their journeys through the earlier worlds; their peccadillos along the way; the endless disapproval they met with; the enduring search for order and beauty and harmony; and the utterly personal way in which such harmony must be expressed and lived. But such harmony is played out, of necessity, in its own times, and there are times when attitudes, actions, and politically correct notions differed from those we imagine to pertain today. For example, the Hopis will never really forgive the Navajos for raiding the village of Oraibi for food, livestock, and slaves in the 1830s, scattering the populace. Memories are long in such small communities everywhere on the planet. But the Navajos will not forget that when the first European showed up, he had already been to the Hopi mesas and had with him Navajos whom the Hopis had held captive. Chicken and egg – an easier matter for biologists to sort out than for historians, and perhaps ultimately fruitless. Lately, some Hopis and some Navajos are beginning to see that they are more alike than they are different when held up to the mirror of what is called the dominant culture, and quite possibly a new adaptation (on both sides) is about to take place; who knows?

In any event, when U.S. Army general Stephen W. Kearny arrived in the territory of New Mexico, technically called a "department" at the time since it was under military administration, and still including the lands we call Arizona, he realized that he had on his hands the Navajos. Among his first public statements to New Mexicans was that his government would "keep off the Indians, protect you in person and property." But Kearny believed that this goal could be achieved, at least so far as the Navajos were concerned, by treaty. He sent forth officers and troops into Navajo country to talk peace and they returned with treaties, in particular one bearing the marks of two Navajo leaders from the western end of Navajo lands – Zarcilla Largo (also known as Jose in some accounts) and Narbona. But, of course, these two leaders spoke for only a hundred or so local Navajos, not the seven thousand it is estimated roamed their extensive territory at the time. (There were, it has been estimated, between five and six thousand Navajo slaves living with New Mexican families.) As a result, raids and counter-raids continued in spite of the treaty.

In the next three years, five separate U.S. government expeditions, guided and assisted by "enemy" Navajos, various pueblo people, and Utes, roamed Navajoland but were never engaged, the Navajos having no interest in fighting for its own sake. Eventually, on August 31, 1849, troops under the command of Colonel John Washington found some Navajo leaders willing to talk peace, among them Largo and Narbona. As the talks concluded, a Mexican working for the American troops claimed that the Navajos had stolen a horse from him and demanded its return. The Navajos refused, and as they turned to leave the order to fire was given. Narbona and six others were killed as the rest fled under artillery fire.

Narbona's death (there are records that he was shot repeatedly and scalped) did nothing to make Navajos more trustful, and it especially outraged Narbona's son-in-law, a rising young war chief of several communities east of the Chuska Mountains, a man called Man of Blackweed and perhaps better known as Manuelito. Meanwhile, a new treaty was signed (at Chinle, near Canyon de Chelly), again by Zarcilla (or Jose) Largo, and this was ratified by the United States and was just as unbinding on most Navajos as the others.

Raid and counterraid between Navajos and the largely Hispanic population of northern New Mexico alternated with periods of calm. More often than not it was Navajos who were less well off who raided the Hispanics, while the better-off Navajos (those with an amplitude of such things as horses or orchards) were essentially the peace party. On the other hand, it was typically the better-off Navajos who were raided by the Hispanics and, thus impoverished, they would swell the ranks of the warlike.

What the Navajos would see of American policy for the next years would be, if nothing else, confusing. In 1851, alarmed by continuing Navajo raids, the War Department established Fort Defiance on the western periphery of Navajo country, with six companies of infantry, cavalry, and artillery. Then, in 1853, a new Indian agent, Captain Henry Linn Dodge, established his residence at Sheep Springs, just north of Fort Defiance (the previous Navajo agent having operated out of Jemez). Dodge was extremely sympathetic to the Navajos and believed that they wanted peace.

He imported a blacksmith and began teaching the working of metal, himself marrying a Navajo woman. This happened to coincide with the stint at Fort Defiance of Major Henry L. Kendrick, also sympathetic to the Navajo, and a period of fairly widespread peace did ensue.

On one occasion, in 1854, Major Kendrick wrote to the governor of New Mexico protesting the invasion of flocks of non-Navajo sheep onto Navajo grazing areas, and pointing out that this would undermine his and Agent Dodge's efforts for peace. The governor, David Meriwether, was also sympathetic, but this happy combination soon came to an end. Dodge was killed by Apaches on a hunting trip in 1856, and a year later Major Kendrick was reassigned to West Point. A Captain William Brooks, a vehemently anti-Navajo man with a short temper, became commanding officer of Fort Defiance, and soon all hell broke loose.

Captain Brooks set aside a large area for grazing the fort's horses, which local Navajos took as a ruthless appropriation of what they had long considered an important pastureland. Navajo horses in that area were shot and, in retaliation, so was a black slave owned by Major Brooks. The commander demanded that Zarcilla Largo give up the murderer. In customary fashion Largo offered blood money, which was refused. He then offered up the body of a Mexican slave of the Navajos. This ruse didn't work, and Brooks made sufficient of the incident that war was soon officially declared on the Navajos.

There is evidence that Brooks's lower-ranking officers thought that Brooks was acting impetuously and putting too many demands on the Navajos. A Captain Walker wrote that "before severe measures are resolved on and a course of policy initiated that would entail poverty and wretchedness upon the entire tribe, it may be that some little forebearance would be the better part of true wisdom." Others pointed out that treaties that had been imposed on Navajos bound them "to make restitution, but leaves them without redress for injuries inflicted upon them" by both New Mexicans and other Indian tribes. Nevertheless, the brass went ahead with a military campaign that in 1859 saw American troops, aided by members of virtually all other nearby tribes, roaming the length and breadth of Navajoland. No Navajo surrendered, a few were killed (apparently peaceful ones), and Navajo counterraids continued unabated, particularly in the east. Largo and others, including a man named Ganado Mucho (evidently referring to his great wealth of sheep), continued to counsel peace, but Manuelito and others, including a man named Barboncito (Little Beard), planned an outright attack on Fort Defiance, where victory, it was hoped, would drive the white man out of Navajo territory.

In April 1860, some two thousand Navajo warriors swept down on the fort. Armed mostly with bows and arrows, though some had rifles, they were certainly the largest group of Navajo warriors ever assembled in one place. There is some evidence that they almost succeeded in taking the fort but after two hours the artillery proved too much and the Navajos were driven off. Large numbers were wounded and killed. Though they had lost at Fort Defiance, Navajos, spurred on by Manuelito, continued and even extended their raids with renewed vigor. New Mexican "volunteers" (meaning slave-raiders) organized counterattacks, in a short period of time taking a reported one hundred women and children as slaves. In July, the War Department ordered active operations against the Navajos *without* the use of volunteers. The head of the New Mexico command at the time, a General E. R. S. Canby, had decided that the Navajos would have to be rounded up and taken a long way from their lands to be reformed.

Then, a most peculiar thing happened. It appeared to Navajos that, despite their loss of the battle at Fort Defiance, they had won the war. In 1861 the fort was abandoned. Troops in the area were withdrawn, with only a token group remaining in Fort Fauntleroy to the east of what is present-day Gallup, New Mexico. Fort Fauntleroy would soon be renamed Fort Wingate when its namesake wound up joining the Confederates. It was, of course the American Civil War that was preoccupying the army, and for two years Navajos felt little interference in their lives from American soldiers. But in the fall of 1862, Brigadier General James H. Carleton was put in charge of the New Mexico command, arriving from California with a column of troops and the assignment to protect the territory from Confederate invasion, subjugate the warlike Indians, and open a mail route. By the time he arrived, the last Confederate threat had evaporated, so he set about implementing his predecessor Canby's plan.

Carleton determined first to establish a military post he called Fort Sumner (known also as Bosque Redondo) along the Little Pecos River in eastern New Mexico. This would be the place to relocate the Navajos – in his words, "a spacious tribal reformatory, away from the haunts and hills and hiding places of their country." A board of officers was dispatched to the designated reformatory and recommended to Carleton that he choose another spot, this one having poor water, poor wood supplies, and the threat of floods. But Carleton's mind was made up. Second, he determined to start not with the Navajos but with the Mescalero Apaches to the south and placed Colonel Christopher (Kit) Carson in command of seven hundred volunteers from New Mexico. Carson, a former trapper and mountain man, had served as an Indian agent in the region, resigning to join the Union Army only to protect the territory against Confederates. He was reluctant to fight Indians in general, but led the foray against the Mescalero, which ended five months later with most of them (about four hundred) surrendering and being herded to Bosque Redondo.

With this victory under his belt, General Carleton held a meeting in northern New Mexico (in a slave-raiding town called Cubero) with some "peaceful" Navajo leaders, offering them land in Bosque Redondo and rations until they got on their feet as farmers. A few took him up on his offer, but Manuelito and Barboncito and others, still believing that they were stronger than the Americans – evidenced by the abandoning of Fort Defiance – announced that they had no intention of leaving their homeland. And so it was up to Kit Carson – Red Shirt, as the Navajos came to call him – to implement Carleton's policy, which in a letter to Carson he described thusly:

Say to them, 'Go to the Bosque Redondo, or we will pursue you and destroy you. We will not make peace with you on any other terms. You have deceived us too often and robbed and murdered our people too long – to trust you again at large in your own country. This war will be pursued against you if it takes years . . . until you cease to exist or move.'

Carleton had earlier (in June) ordered the commanding officer at Fort Wingate to tell the Navajos, that they had until July 20, 1863, to come in and surrender. After that they would be considered hostile "and treated accordingly." Of course, there was no conceivable way to notify Navajos who lived scattered throughout some thirty thousand square miles, so in effect Carleton was declaring an open season on all of them. And, precisely on July 20, Kit Carson arrived to reestablish Fort Defiance as his headquarters. Almost immediately he began military operations. These consisted chiefly of a scorched earth policy, the attempt to deprive Navajos in his path of any means of livelihood or survival. Cornfields were systematically destroyed, peach trees cut down, sheep by the thousands slaughtered and left to rot. And people were killed. In the campaign of 1863, chiefly an autumnal affair, some 300 Navajos were killed, about 90 wounded and 700 captured. In all, about 40 of Carson's men were casualties, with seventeen killed. By the turn of the year, as Carson would later relate, "owing to the operations of my command, they are in a complete state of starvation . . . many of their women and children have already died from this cause."

The final and humiliating military blow followed in January. Many Navajos had found a stronghold/hiding place in the depths of Canyon de Chelly, a magnificent red sandstone gash in the earth north and west of Fort Wingate. Carson sent troops defiantly marching from end to end through the fields and sandy riverbed of the canyon, corralling sheep and destroying farms and orchards. Navajos, shooting arrows from the rim of the canyon, were helpless to stop this depredation, and it signaled the end. The Navajos simply lost the spirit to resist in the face of this relentless and destructive pursuit by a superior force.

Within two months, some six thousand Navajos were in camps near Fort Wingate and Fort Defiance, preparatory to being sent to Bosque Redondo. Carson had brought superior force and had destroyed any hope for a livelihood for the People in his path. But also, contrary to Carleton's draconian cut-off date (after which any Navajo was to be considered hostile and shot), Carson was relatively generous in his treatment of those who surrendered, providing them with much-needed rations in their camps around the forts. Still, some Navajos died in the camps.

In February and March of that year, 1864, a series of deportations began that came to be called the Long Walk, the most traumatic event in all of the Navajos' association with other people in their history. This, the penultimate step in the implementation of General Carleton's plan to "civilize" the Navajos, can be better comprehended if it is put in some historical perspective. It took place far away from the major concerns of most people in the country and the world, at a time when Indian affairs were pursued through the War Department of the United States and the chief argument about such affairs seesawed back and forth between two alternatives: the Christianization of Indians either on reserves or by absorption, or their outright destruction.

Most American Indians were seen even in enlightened and scholarly circles in Western society as "savages," which meant that they were a big step below the next highest stage of human evolution: "barbarism," a state of sedentary agriculturalism in which certain pueblo tribes existed. In this year, Abraham Lincoln was reelected president, Ulysses S. Grant was made commander-in-chief of the Union Army, and after some battles between Grant and Lee, it was by no means clear who would win the Civil War. In America, slaves had been officially emancipated for a year. In 1864, Dickens published his last novel and H. G. Wells came out with *A Journey to the Center of the Earth*. Louis Pasteur suggested a method to keep wine from spoiling that would soon lead to the pasteurization of milk, and a British scientist found that electromagnetic waves travel at the speed of light. A Geneva Convention established that in the wars between civilized nations battlefield medical facilities were neutral territory.

It was in this stage of Western civilization's grand progress that, in all, some 8,500 Navajo men, women, and children were torn from their lands and traditions and their gods and sent on foot on a trek some 300 miles overland to Fort Sumner, the dreaded Hweeldi in Navajo parlance, to learn, in Carleton's words, "the arts of peace" and "the truths of Christianity." There they would acquire the skills of the pueblo farmer and cease to be "nomads," and, as the old ones "die off and carry with them all latent longings for murdering and robbing," they would become "the happiest and most delightfully located pueblo of Indians in New Mexico – perhaps in the United States." Instead, it came close to being genocide by U.S. government policy.

Counting those who died at the forts while waiting (there had been no medical facilities in this war), more than three hundred Navajos died in the first two convoys to Fort Sumner – more than ten percent of those involved. Dysentery and frostbite and fatigue took some. Stragglers were picked off by New Mexican slave raiders along the way while soldiers looked on; it is claimed that complainers were summarily shot. Indeed, Howard Gorman, at one time a member of the Navajo Tribal Council, recalled stories he had been told by his older relatives and related one incident where the army would not allow a pause in the march for a young woman to give birth. She paused anyway and was shot by one of the soldiers.

Most of the Navajos probably had no idea why they were being rounded up and sent off to some unknown place; many assumed it was to be put to death. If indeed a few of their people had acted to incur American antagonism, why did they all have to be punished? In fact, all Navajos weren't punished by taking the Long Walk. Some, as noted, escaped this fate by being picked off and sold into slavery. Others, some estimates say as many as two thousand, escaped into the fastnesses of the Grand Canyon, Navajo Mountain in Utah, perhaps even into the lands of the Chiricahua Apaches. One diehard, war leader Manuelito, withdrew far to the west with a band of Navajos, but he eventually surrendered to the soldiers in September 1866, and the "Navajo Wars" were effectively over.

Out of the tragic years at Hweeldi, nothing that General Carleton had planned for occurred except, perhaps ironically, the one thing he might have deplored had he known with whom he was dealing in the first place.

Carleton's spacious reformatory was a failure from the start. In all, more than 8,000 Navajos were crammed into the grounds of the fort along with 400 Mescalero Apaches and 400 soldiers. The soldiers gave out rations and regularly counted the prisoners, and were under orders to teach them how to build pueblo-style houses. The Navajos took the rations, submitted to the regular head counts, but made no effort to learn adobe construction, nor did they put any effort into planting the irrigated fields that had been prepared for them. Instead of adobe houses (which they had once tried out and rejected), they dug round pit houses and covered them with branches. Supplies such as blankets and firewood were inadequate; many of the Navajos couldn't adjust to the rations (or the poor water) and dysentery was common. A smallpox epidemic in 1865 took more than two thousand Navajo lives in short order. Corrupt agents skimming rations and supplies made matters even worse. Quarrels erupted with the Apaches who, in fact, simply left in 1865 and were not brought back. Other Indians made occasional raids on the prisoners, and Navajos began sneaking off.

Martial law prevailed in the Territory until 1865, but after the Civil War ended, so did martial law. People began to take note of the unraveling of Carleton's experiment and a few critics became vocal. Joseph Knapp, who had lost his job as a member of the Territorial Supreme Court in 1864 over his disagreement with Carleton's reformatory, attacked the entire plan in an open letter to an area newspaper. He accused Carleton of illegally declaring war on the Navajos, and of improperly making an entire tribe responsible for the acts of a few. "Old men and women too decrepit to walk," he wrote, "little ones equally, yes more helpless, women and children, noncombatants, and those not able to take care of themselves much less to fight, are all held as prisoners of war. . . . Where do you find the rule for such conduct? Certainly not in any code of civilized warfare."

Others had more pragmatic complaints. Some objected to the high costs of maintaining the Navajos at Bosque Redondo (some $2 million dollars a year), while others with cattle interests coveted the place as rangeland. Still others were simply nervous about so great a concentration of Indians in eastern New Mexico. Meanwhile, from 1864 to 1867, what crops were planted failed consistently owing to drought and grasshoppers, and disease continued to plague the prisoners. Carleton was relieved as commander of the Department of New Mexico in 1866, and the following year the responsibility for the Navajos was taken out of the War Department and given to the Bureau of Indian Affairs. In November 1867, an investigation of Bosque Redondo yielded a report recommending that the wholly failed experiment in acculturation be abandoned. Congress established a commission that same year with the goal of making peace with various tribes, and in May 1868, led by General William T. Sherman, it arrived at Fort Sumner to make a treaty with the Navajos.

Throughout the four-year ordeal, the Navajos had continued their ceremonies in an effort to create *hozho* out of the awful chaos of Hweeldi, and their persistence in these practices is widely credited with keeping the People from the brink of total despair. And when the peace commission came to Fort Sumner, still uncertain about where the Navajos should be sent – possibly to Texas or the Indian Territory (now Oklahoma) – Barboncito told them, "I hope to God you will not ask me to go to any other country but my own." And, apparently, Barboncito also led the People in a special ceremony called Put a Bead in Coyote's Mouth. In short, a coyote within a circle of people was caught by Barboncito, who put a piece of white shell in its mouth and released it. The coyote turned clockwise from east to west and walked off in that direction, and Barboncito said that it meant the People would be set free.

And indeed a treaty was drawn up, allowing the Navajos to return to their original territory, a rectangular reservation lying athwart what is now the Arizona – New Mexico border – in all, approximately one-tenth the area which they had formerly inhabited. Signed by Barboncito, Manuelito, Ganado Mucho and several others on June 1, 1868, and ratified by Congress the following month, the treaty also called for the Navajos to send their children to schools the government would establish. The government promised to supply rations as needed for ten years while the People got back on their feet, and also – once they were resettled – to provision them with livestock. On June 18, a column of Navajos ten miles long headed home, escorted by four companies of U.S. Cavalry. The four-year ordeal was over. The wounds in the minds of the Navajo would heal, but the scars would remain as a bitter tribal memory never to be forgotten. Navajo life would never be the same as it had been before the Long Walk.

During the period at Fort Sumner, the officers had broken the People up into twelve groups, each with a designated headman. The twelve headmen formed a council with whom the officers could deal. It has been pointed out that at Bosque Redondo and in the entire Long Walk era, the government dealt with the Navajos as one people and, in the enforced association with one another, the shared experience of anguish and deprivation, the Navajos began to view themselves as a single political unit, not just a group of people with a common language and other shared cultural traits. A new kind of unity – a common political identity – had willy-nilly been forged in the crucible of Hweeldi and the Long Walk, what might be called in hindsight the first rootlets of a plant that would become known as the Navajo Nation, a nation within a nation. This plant of nationalistic feeling would grow in fits and starts over the next decades, but it would take another catastrophic run-in with the U.S. government for it to begin truly to flower.

A Navajo Nation

A joyous return in 1868 from imprisonment at Fort Sumner to their new/old lands was tempered by the fact that, being too late to plant and without livestock, the Navajos had to rely totally on government rations to get them through the winter. In the spring, the government made good, handing out 14,000 sheep and 1,000 goats to some 9,500 Navajos, plus another 10,000 sheep three years later. Some 2,500 Navajos settled around Fort Defiance, but the rest fanned out into the reservation. Some moved beyond the reservation, seeking good forage for their livestock or nothing more than their previous homes. Within eleven years of their return, the Dineh occupied, in addition to their 3½-million acre reservation, some 6 million adjacent acres.

While most tribal populations declined, the Navajo population grew rapidly, from 15,000 in 1870 to 30,000 in the early twentieth century. And with it, the livestock herds grew at a rapid rate. The Navajos became largely self-sufficient, leading traditional lives in their largely untrammeled land, supplementing their incomes as needed by the sale of craft items such as silver and turquoise jewelry and weaving. Some took an occasional paying job with the railroad (the Atlantic and Pacific, later called the Santa Fe), which began pushing through in the 1880s. Livestock as the basic way of life was encouraged as well by the government agents of the time.

While some Navajo herdsmen eventually took up the nomadic life that General Carleton thought typical of Navajos (and deplored), most of Navajo society settled into a pattern of decentralized sedentary pastoralism, with children often serving as shepherds. A herd of sheep would include those owned by various members of the extended family, including fairly young children. In tending their own sheep and those owned by other family members, children were socialized into the delicate balance between individual autonomy and communalism that is a Navajo characteristic to this day. During the first half century of reservation life, government agents did little to dissuade the Navajos from their beliefs and lifeways, as they did among most other tribes. For example, so isolated were the Navajos from the outside world, that only about one percent of the People spoke English in 1898.

But the outside world did impinge on, and gradually begin to make significant economic changes among, the Navajo. This came about through a relatively small group of Anglos – traders. The first trading post on Navajoland was established in 1870, and by 1900 there were nearly eighty trading posts on or near the reservation, all licensed to operate there by the U.S. government under certain rules that ensured fair practices (which were sometimes overlooked). From the growing livestock herds, such products as wool, hides, meat, and woven rugs began to find their way to the marketplace. In return, the Navajo began to receive products from the

Dressed in his finest silver and turquoise, a tribal judge attends the Navajo Nation's annual fair at Window Rock.

Anglo culture that they increasingly desired – furniture, household equipment, Anglo clothing. Indeed, by the 1930s, some 150 traders had virtually replaced the traditional subsistence economy of barter among Navajos and with other tribes. A trader would settle in one or another community and extend credit to the Navajos, whose herds produced trade goods only two times a year – wool in spring, lambs in the fall. To this, women added rugs, the designs of which the traders increasingly influenced, with their eyes fixed on Anglo tastes. Typically, credit could be secured by holding Navajos' jewelry as pawn, though many traders would let debtors use the pawned jewelry for major events. The arrangement was similar to traditional Navajo transactions – oral agreement, a long-term relationship made up of many transactions, and generally a flexible schedule for repayment of debts. Thus were Navajos edged from a subsistence economy to something resembling a commercial one. In this period, the local trader was the only point of contact with the outside world of commerce and this could – and did – lead to certain abuses. Some traders charged exorbitant interest and were free to put huge markups on the Navajo goods they sold, thus often getting rich while the Navajos themselves remained poor.

On the other hand, many of the traders exercised a benevolent and sympathetic influence on the reservation. One of these, Lorenzo Hubbell, scion of a prominent western entrepreneurial family, acted throughout much of the first half of this century as a crucial buffer between Navajos (and Hopis) and the rest of the world from his post in Oraibi. His story has been hauntingly chronicled in *West of the Thirties,* a memoir of his years on the reservation before World War II by anthropologist Edward T. Hall. Hubbell dealt with his Navajo and Hopi clients with a scrupulous honesty and was more often than not the only person who could explain the wayward and incomprehensible actions of the local Indian agency to the bewildered Indians, in some instances preventing violence by his intercession. Navajos who pawned jewelry to Hubbell in return for either cash or needed goods might wait for years before reclaiming it, and Hubbell would display it in his trading post so that the Indian would know it was still there, never selling it until the owner had either died or moved away. (Hubbell's trading post near Ganado is now a National Monument.)

The traders continued to be a powerful economic, cultural, and political force on the reservation until after World War II, when automobiles began to be prevalent and the Navajos gained access to places beyond their own community.

The only effort the government made to civilize the Navajo was to provide them with schools that would teach, among other things, the English language. Despite agreeing in the treaty to send their children to the government schools, Navajo parents saw little use in it. They knew how to make a living and how to live properly in the world already; they didn't like the kind of draconian discipline they saw in the Anglo schools; and, furthermore, they needed the children at home to tend the sheep. So they sent slave children or orphans, and kept those with potential at home. This form of resistance was typically passive, though it did lead to a few noisy fracases over the years. By the turn of the century, only about three percent of

At the Piñon trading post, as elsewhere on the reservation, winter can turn the world to mud.

Navajo children attended school and, even as late as 1930, only forty percent were in school. (Later, the Navajos would become truly interested in obtaining a school education for their children, but it would not be until the 1950s that the government provided sufficient classroom space for all Navajo children.)

As for the land provided for the Navajo, it had been no great sacrifice when the government defined the original reservation. It was federal land that no one at the time particularly wanted. And from 1878 to 1886, five additions were made to the original reservation, including an executive order in 1882 that authorized a reservation for the Hopi and others whom the Secretary of Interior might designate. (The Navajos, the only other Indians in the neighborhood, presumed that they had been so designated, and this would lead to a bitter land dispute almost a century later.) Other additions to the Navajo Reservation would be made over the years, more than quadrupling the original amount of land.

As the Navajos expanded, both in numbers and in land extent, they ran into an expanding Anglo-American population which was beginning to settle in the Southwest, as well as Mormons who were moving into southern Utah. There were misunderstandings and some outright clashes. In 1897, for example, sixteen families were living, as had their forebears, in a heretofore unsurveyed tract of land near the Colorado River in Arizona's Coconino County. In January, a sheriff's posse arrived to demand a fee of $5 for every one hundred sheep owned. The Navajos were without cash of any sort and the posse proceeded to drive them away, having rounded up their herds and burned their houses and corrals. As the Commissioner of Indian Affairs reported: "they and their flocks were rounded up and pushed north toward the Little Colorado River with relentless haste, the posse keeping women, children, and animals in fright by an intermittent fire from rifles and revolvers. When the river was reached it was found to be so deep as to require the sheep to swim. The posse surrounded the flocks and pushed them into the water, and nearly all the lambs, with many grown sheep, went down the stream or froze to death after crossing, and many died afterward from the effects of exposure."

The commissioner later ruled that the fee the sheriff had demanded of the Navajos for the right to graze their sheep was "unlawful," but many settlers and their local governments continued to feel free to interpret laws their own way. The Navajos had little idea what they were talking about. For example, Navajos found that they were as entitled as anyone to take up private ownership of nonreservation lands under the provisions of the Homestead Act, but land agents uniformly disqualified hogans as improper structures and no Navajo homesteads were recorded.

Overall, however (and particularly in comparison with other tribes around the nation), the Navajo fared well in the latter part of the nineteenth century. Navajo culture began to penetrate the minds of many Americans in this era, in great part through the efforts of the traders. With the death of the old leaders, like Manuelito and Barboncito, the Navajo political structure reverted almost completely to the loose arrangements that had pertained before the Long Walk. This fractionation was abetted further in the first decade of the twentieth century when the federal government broke the reservation up into five agencies, with a headquarters in each, the idea being to create a more systematic administration of Navajo affairs. Later, the Bureau of Indian Affairs would encourage the creation of chapters, political units rather like tiny counties, where local matters, disputes, and public works projects could be discussed.

Today, the chapters are a vital part of the Navajo political fabric, handling numerous local affairs and each sending a delegate to the Tribal Council. Until the second decade of this century, there was no central Navajo tribal body and the pressure for its creation was almost totally applied from outside. Prospectors probing reservation lands (much to the distress of the Navajos) had begun to find deposits of various valuable metals on Navajoland, and in 1918, the U.S. Congress passed the Metalliferous Minerals Leasing Act, permitting mining on Indian lands by outside people, and providing for a royalty of five percent to the tribe in question. Then oil leasing was similarly authorized.

In 1923, the Secretary of the Interior issued rules establishing a Navajo Tribal Council, consisting of an elected chairman, vice-chairman, and delegates from each of the five agencies. The intention was to provide the government with a Navajo entity with which it could deal. The first meeting of the council was held in Toadlena, New Mexico, in July 1923, and gave the newly appointed commissioner of the Navajo tribe the power to sign mineral leases on behalf of the tribe. A carrot was held out, as it would be many times, to obtain this blank check: the suggestion that cooperation with the government was the only way to obtain additional lands for the reservation. Much of the land in this remote part of the southwest was owned by the U.S. government or the two states and was not considered a particularly valuable economic asset, being mostly high desert scrublands. At the time, this council, whose members served at the pleasure of the Interior Department, had little to do with the day-to-day lives of the great majority of the Navajo people, but this would soon change.

As early as the 1880s, there had been some mention of overgrazing by the burgeoning livestock herds. In the twenties, it was becoming evident to more and more people (largely Anglos involved in administering Navajo affairs) that the reservation lands were eroding at an alarming rate.

Government agents on the reservation sought to ameliorate what was clearly (to them) a severe overgrazing problem by building a few hundred wells and reservoirs, encouraging voluntary stock reduction and selective breeding of sheep with what was taken to be superior stock. The Navajos would have none of the latter two notions, but some eventually reduced their stock of horses to satisfy the government to some extent, in the hopes of obtaining additional land.

By the thirties, the Depression had lowered prices for the products of livestock, Dustbowl conditions had arrived, and the liberal, reform-minded Commissioner of Indian Affairs, John Collier, determined that the best way to perpetuate Navajo culture, which he admired, was to bring about both a major reduction of Navajo stock and an increase in their lands. With the usual tactics, this idea was bulldozed through the Navajo Tribal Council, which voted unanimously for stock reduction on being promised (by federal officials) additional land from both Arizona and New Mexico. Meanwhile, most Navajos saw the problem of soil erosion as little more than the result of drought conditions (which would change in due course). Sheep reduction, for many Navajos, was akin to losing one's limbs, so central to both economic and ceremonial life had sheep become.

Nevertheless, in 1934, a stock-reduction program was put in force. Those Navajos with large amounts of sheep simply volunteered their culls; smaller herds were devastated. This would later be changed to a percentage reduction for all herds – forty percent but by then a great deal of damage had been done. Even the Superintendent of Navajo admitted that "In all honesty the Navajos have every reason to fear and misunderstand land management. The previous adjustment program was certainly unfair to smaller owners."

Only belatedly did the government attempt to educate the People about the need for reduction. Instead, for most it simply came out of the blue, and was done by force, not persuasion. Since there was little market for the livestock (which the government purchased from the Navajos), they were mostly just shot and allowed to rot in place. Virtually every Navajo on the reservation was left with the mental image of government agents slaughtering their treasured animals. This has since been called the single greatest disaster the Navajos experienced after the Long Walk.

It was Collier's doing, most Navajos thought, and when New Mexico interests summarily blocked Collier's attempt to provide the Navajos with any additional land, as Collier had unwisely promised the Navajos, they felt doubly betrayed by him. He was quickly placed in the Navajos' pantheon of evildoers, along with General Carleton and Colonel Carson. More than that, however, relations in general between the Navajos and the federal government became badly strained, with the Navajos harboring a deep-seated suspicion of Washington and its works. The tribe resoundingly voted down participation in the Indian Reorganization Act, by which Collier sought to have each tribal group adopt a government-drafted constitution. The Navajo submitted their own, which Collier rejected. Instead, he issued a set of rules under which the Navajo Tribal Council would henceforth operate. These included a secret ballot and the election of seventy-four delegates in place of what had by then grown to twelve. Meanwhile, the five administrative districts had been merged into one centered in Window Rock, Arizona. And even though the earlier council had acquiesced in the devastating stock-reduction plan (as would later ones through the forties), Navajos began to realize that these leaders had little choice in the matter. They also, however, began to realize that it was to the Tribal Council and not to the unpredictable government in Washington that they had best look. A sense of a Navajo Nation was in the air.

Pine Hill is a prosperous community in the wooded high country of Ramah, a separate part of the Navajo Reservation that lies to the south and the east of the Zuni Reservation in New Mexico. In 1989, a Navajo couple, Mary and Bennie Cohoe, were sponsors of an Indian children's rodeo, one of many that take place around the Navajo and other reservations in the Southwest every summer. (Rodeo is extremely popular among the Navajos, many of whom enjoy being both cowboys and Indians.) Bennie Cohoe is

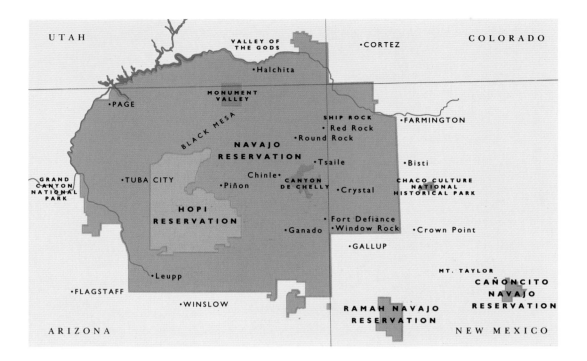

a cattle rancher and principal of the local high school; Mary was at the time working for the Navajo tribe in Window Rock – a long daily commute – and had previously been instrumental in creating a local radio station.

Susanne and I drove out to Ramah for the rodeo, having in tow a young friend, Adam Klein from New York, who had recently graduated from the University of Indiana's opera school and who had never been to a rodeo or an Indian reservation. We introduced Adam to Mary Cohoe, mentioning that he was an opera singer, and Mary immediately asked him if he would like to sing the national anthem in the rodeo's opening ceremony. Adam gulped, agreed, and about an hour later climbed the rickety stairs to the announcer's booth above the rodeo grounds. The announcer, a regular on the kid's circuit named Cliff Ami (a Hopi), began with a long prayer to which the hundred-odd spectators listened attentively, and then announced that the spectators would now hear "the most beautiful song in the world," the national anthem, but a special version of it, since they were lucky enough to have on hand, all the way from New York, Mr. Adam "Clean", an opera singer. Adam chose to sing it straight, not in an operatic voice, but thanks to his training he phrased those often-heard lyrics in such a way that they had real meaning. His voice, mighty in the loudspeakers, belted out across the hills, taking the later (and for most people impossible) high notes as easily as Middle C, and when he was finished, there was a period of many seconds of absolute silence. No one present, none of the Navajos, nor Cliff Ami, nor Susanne nor I, had ever heard the national anthem sung so perfectly: people were stunned.

Prolonged applause followed, and throughout the afternoon Cliff Ami would periodically remind the audience of "Mr. Clean's" stirring rendition and there would be more applause. Strange as it may seem for a people who were vanquished, put in what amounts to a concentration camp and otherwise pushed around by the United States government, Navajos are unreservedly patriotic. (The government has also been helpful to them in many ways, of which they are mindful, but their palpable patriotism does not seem to be a calculated matter at all.) They make a special point of publicly honoring their war veterans. The long prayer that preceded the anthem had dwelled upon those veterans present, particularly the elder ones, from World War II – the old warriors, the code talkers, now in their sixties and seventies.

World War II was, in fact, a major turning point in recent Navajo history. In all, 3,600 of the People served in the armed forces, some in the European theater but most in the Pacific. Even before Pearl Harbor, the Tribal Council had passed a resolution that said, "the Navajo Indians stand ready as they did in 1918 to aid and defend our Government and its institutions against all subversive and armed conflict." The idea for the code talkers – the use of the complex language of the Navajos as a "code" for military communication on the battlefield and elsewhere – came from the son of a reservation missionary. Soon the U.S. Marines had recruited some 450 Navajos (and some from other tribes). The code proved to be unbreakable.

But beyond men and women in the armed forces, some twelve thousand Navajos became employed on the home front in the war effort – in off-reservation jobs in agriculture and industry. In short, about half of all adult Navajos at the time were engaged in largely new pursuits, seeing the outside world as few had before. Importantly, a number of Navajos had found that they did not qualify for military service because their use of English was insufficient. The postwar effects were far-reaching. There arose in the tribe a desire for universal schooling for Navajo children, along with a desire for many of the things and services that were common in the Anglo world. Many who returned found no need on the reservation for the skills they had learned, and within a few years poverty was widespread. The federal government and the states responded with aid of various kinds, especially education programs and economic development programs – in particular, the building of roads in the reservation where dirt tracks over the endless spaces had been the norm.

At the same time Republicans had won the majority of seats in Congress in 1946, and the policy of "termination" began to take root: essentially, the notion that Indians should become self-sufficient citizens like everyone else, with the ultimate dissolution of the reservation system and of the special (and expensive) relationship between Indian tribes and the U.S. government. It was obvious to many Navajos that if the federal government's role was to diminish, they had to look to their own government to supply essential services to the People. And happily, beginning in the 1950s, a series of oil discoveries on the reservation began putting unprecedentedly large amounts of money in the tribal coffers. Coal deposits could also be developed, and with the vaunted promise of atomic energy for peaceful purposes, uranium deposits on the reservation were also greatly sought. From this activity, Navajos would reap a bitter harvest indeed.

Uranium often occurs in association with vanadium, a metal useful in hardening steel. Vanadium had been found and widely mined on Navajo land in the decades before World War II. During the war, to supply the top-secret Manhattan Project that was under way to develop an atomic bomb, uranium was taken from Navajo vanadium ore deposits. Because of the secrecy of the whole affair, the Navajos never received any royalty for the uranium – only payments for vanadium. After the war, uranium mining became a big business on the reservation and elsewhere in the Southwest. Large companies like Kerr-McGee contracted to supply the Atomic Energy Commission, and uranium mining and milling boomed.

Navajos were given preferential treatment in hiring – which seems only fair – but they were, at the same time, not warned of any of the dangers of handling uranium (dangers that were already known). Nor was anything but the slightest effort made to reduce these dangers. The miners were not given respirators, for example, and most of the mining practices were primitive – men wielding shovels and wheelbarrows. One result of this was that Navajo miners and millworkers (along with their white counterparts) began dying from radiation-related causes in the 1970s. It would not be until the 1990s that the U.S. government took any responsibility for this carelessness, and then only reluctantly began paying compensation to the bereft families. By 1994, approximately half of the claims had been paid.

The story of the last forty years is that of the tribe taking more and more control over its own destiny. This process has always been a struggle, beset with occasional losses and frequent controversy, but in general it is a story of remarkable success. Often progress came about through reaction to outside pressures. A case in point is the tribal judicial system, which the tribe created when faced with the threat that the states would fill the vacuum. Traditionally among the Navajo, as among many tribal people, there was no one filling the role of what we would think of as a judge, deciding things between two individuals. In a dispute between two Navajos, both of their extended families were involved, and this group got together to try to resolve the issue. If they couldn't, they took it to one or more of the respected members of the community, who would serve as mediators. More often than not, after days while everyone had his or her say and the mediator exhorted, advised, and instructed about Navajo traditions, a consensus was reached, and some form of payment (usually not money) ended the matter; *hozho* was restored.

But as the Navajos became more and more embroiled in a nontraditional, wage economy, such a means of resolving conflicts became less useful. (By 1960, for example, about seventy percent of Navajo individual income came from wages, mostly earned from jobs with the tribal or federal government, and less than ten percent from livestock and farming.) And with wages came more and more cash transactions, in particular with non-Navajo operations such as auto dealers and other retail businesses.

In the 1950s there was a Navajo judicial system – for handling petty criminal problems. Appointed by federal officials, the judges had no formal legal training and government officials reviewed their decisions. But when a trader sued a Navajo couple in an Arizona state court, the Tribal Council protested to the U.S. Supreme Court, and at the same time took on responsibility for paying the costs of all law enforcement on the reservation. The council created a new court system to handle such on-reservation problems. The Supreme Court subsequently gave the new Navajo system broad jurisdiction over criminal and civil suits brought against Navajos by outsiders.

Today there are seven judicial district courts and a Navajo Supreme

Court, a system increasingly populated with people of increasing legal sophistication. But there are differences. The new system permitted the creation of "peacemaker" courts that would adjudicate internal matters in much the way of traditional mediation. In some rural areas of the reservation, traditional means of resolving disputes are still resorted to – an ancient process called talking things out. In this process, people who could not resolve a dispute themselves would apply to a respected clan or family member to listen and guide the disputants toward an agreement acceptable to both, thus restoring harmony in the community.

The peacemaker courts established in 1985, with one such court in each of the reservation's seven judicial districts, operate in a similar manner, often with a mediator appointed by a judge. The parties with a problem are joined by various members of their families, who sit in a circle (which is symbolic of the Navajo common law and tradition and is the heart of the peacemaker court). The circle is surrounded by four walls – standing for structure, choice, protection, and enforcement. There are no fees, no lawyers, no deadlines. Instead, the mediator listens to both sides for as long as it takes; once an agreement is reached between the parties, it is recorded by the district court in the proper legal manner. Peacemaker courts can settle disputes about land, vehicles, livestock, divorce, children, and a host of other matters.

As with the judicial system, the Navajos began to take matters into their own hands in education. For decades, many Navajo leaders had recognized the importance of schooling if the People were going to get along in the world they wanted to carve out for themselves on the edge of the Anglo world. Manuelito, the old war leader, had told his grandson Chee Dodge (himself to become a leader in the period of stock reduction): "the whites have many things which we Navajos need. But we cannot get them. It is as though the whites were in a grassy canyon and there they have wagons, plows, and plenty of food. We Navajos are up on the dry mesa. We can hear them talking but we cannot talk to them. My grandchild, education is the ladder. Tell our people to take it."

By the 1950s, the federal government had largely made good on its old promise to supply sufficient schools for all Navajo children. Many of them, however, were boarding schools where children had to be taken far away from their families and communities, in some instances away from Navajoland altogether, and for the better part of a year. (In the 1970s, Susanne came across a notice posted on a rural trading post, drawing attention to the date that the buses would leave to take first-graders off to school. Its headline read, *Final. Shipment.*)

In the 1960s, unhappy with the quality of education supplied by these Bureau of Indian Affairs schools (which had a strongly "assimilationist" attitude, with only English spoken and Navajo or even Indian culture generally not spoken of at all), the Navajos began some of their own schools, notably at Rough Rock, that would be bicultural and run by Navajos. Similarly, they created the Navajo Community College and eventually established it on its own campus near Tsaile, northeast of Chinle. Eventually, they also made arrangements with the federal government and the local counties to provide a network of public schools on the reservation, and diverted a portion of mineral-royalties into a college scholarship program administered by the tribe.

In the course of all this, they sometimes got burned, each time trying to determine the reason for any failure and to gain in expertise. In a hurry to develop the extensive coal deposits on Black Mesa (they had been advised that fossil fuels would soon be a thing of the past, what with atomic energy soon to supply the nation's electricity needs), they made what now seems a hasty arrangement with Peabody Coal Company. They wound up with lower royalty payments than they might have gotten, and agreed to the use of deep underground water resources (to slurry the coal through a pipeline to its ultimate destination) that they were told were brackish. In fact, it was the best water on the reservation. In addition, they trod abruptly on the toes of those Navajos who lived on the land to be mined. They were also apparently utterly unaware of the extent to which such coal development would cause pollution. The massive Four Corners power complex generated a smoke plume that was the only man-made thing that orbiting astronauts saw. The Navajo found themselves causing a nationwide uproar on the part of the then-burgeoning environmental movement.

A more wrenching reverse took place in the highly complex and much-publicized land dispute with the Hopis, a matter that had been simmering for decades. By the sixties, a small lozenge-shaped area called District Six had been established as exclusive Hopi territory, while the remainder of the rectangular reservation (the 1882 Executive Order Reservation) was legally deemed to be "joint use" land for both tribes. Feelings on both sides of this issue were deep and bitter. In the 1970s the U.S. government was beginning to conclude that the joint-use area should be somehow split in two, with half for the Hopis and half for the Navajos. In 1974, a bill emerged from Congress, calling for a six-month period of negotiations between the two tribes, with the help of a federal negotiator, to iron things out. A Navajo official at the time hoped that "left alone without outside intervention by Congress or attorneys, the two tribes could work it out."

But they couldn't, and with both sides equally unhappy, a U.S. District Court judge eventually drew a tortuous line through the joint use territory, partitioning it into equal parts, and calling for the relocation of almost 3,500 Navajos and 40 Hopis. The matter continued to drag on through appeals, congressional action and inaction, presidential vetoes, and continuing bitterness. In due course, in the 1980s, the matter was officially resolved and a Relocation Committee began the painful administration of the required relocations. There continued to be pockets of Navajo resistance, notably in the Big Mountain area. The relocation process continues to this day. In their own eyes, each side was right, and in the denouement, each side feels that it has been deprived of the use of ancestral lands. Both governments, Hopi and Navajo, appear to be resigned to the ultimate implementation of what is to each party an unsatisfactory solution but, under the circumstances, the best either could have obtained.

All the while, the Navajo government had been strengthening itself as the major force in the lives of its people, taking on more and more responsibility for Navajo destiny – as it clearly had to. In 1975, for example, the Tribal Council approved a budget of nearly $23.5 million and then-chairman

Coal miners near Black Hat, east of Window Rock, demonstrate solidarity Navajo-style.

Peter MacDonald was looking forward to a budget of more than twice that the following year because of renegotiation of mineral leases and greater income from other outside sources.

In that same year the U.S. Commission on Civil Rights issued a report to the president, based on an earlier investigation including hearings on the reservation. The report detailed the most flagrant failures of the U.S. government to live up to its obligations to the Navajos. To begin with, the report pointed out, thanks to the murky legal status of the tribal government, Navajos had lost out in federal aid routinely given to other local governments. Tribal governments weren't on the list of governmental bodies that the Federal Highway Administration could assist, so the reservation's ratio of paved roads to square miles was way below par with surrounding areas. In another example, the federal government collected excise taxes on tribal police vehicles, a tax from which state and county governments were exempt. Clarifying the tribal government's legal status was crucial to any hopes of economic development, but the report (titled *The Navajo Nation: An American Colony*) pointed out that "The Federal Government has chosen to run a relief economy rather than a development economy." Federal regulations mitigated against starting new businesses on the reservation, as did federal bureaucratic snafus. For example, nonprofit cooperatives, which seemed more suited to underlying Navajo principles than profit-oriented commerce, could not be funded by the Small Business Administration. In one instance, the SBA approved a loan to start a commercial laundry with the proviso that the Bureau of Indian Affairs guarantee the contract for three years. The BIA said it could make no such guarantee and claimed, furthermore and "without any apparent evidence," that the laundry (to be run in Tuba City, Arizona, on the western side of the reservation) would put another Indian laundry out of business. The other laundry was located some two hundred miles away from Tuba City. Nor, the commission said, did the BIA make any effort to monitor or enforce provisions in contracts between the Navajo tribe and corporations doing business on the reservation that called for preferential hiring of Navajo workers: "no contractor has been sued by the Government for violation of a contract's employment provisions." The BIA's response to Navajo unemployment (then forty percent) was characterized as ranging from "obstructionist to, at best, insufficient to change the status quo."

The commission went on to find that in education, Navajos "have been excluded from the decision-making process," and as a result, "Navajo language and culture have been largely ignored in the curriculum offered to Navajo students." In the matter of health (the responsibility of the Indian Health Service, then in the Department of Health, Education and Welfare), the commission claimed that the "injustice on the Navajo people . . . is one of both nonfeasance and malfeasance." The six IHS hospitals in Navajoland were "critically understaffed" and the commission cited one where newborns were often left unattended, with the result that three infants had died because of inadequate monitoring.

In the intervening years, some of these conditions have improved substantially, others less so (topics of a later chapter). The Navajo Nation has also experienced a good deal of internal political turmoil. Peter MacDonald had served three terms as tribal chairman before being defeated by Petersen Zah in the early 1980s. Four years later, MacDonald was reelected for an unprecedented fourth term. In the Navajo system at this time, the tribal chairman headed the executive branch, had more legislative power in the council than does the speaker of the U.S. House of Representatives, and was as well the representative of the tribe to other governments and the rest of the outside world. But in 1989 a calamity for Navajo pride began to change this political world. MacDonald was accused in U.S. Senate hearings of taking bribes and kickbacks from various contractors. Before long the Tribal Council voted that MacDonald take leave while the charges were investigated, and they appointed an interim chairman, Leonard Haskie, a member of the council. In the ensuing controversy, the Navajo Supreme Court insisted that it was sufficiently independent of political control to review the council's decision, and upheld it. After a violent demonstration in Window Rock in which two people were killed, MacDonald agreed to take leave while his criminal charges worked their way through the tribal courts. (He was convicted.)

Meanwhile, the Tribal Council restructured the executive and legislative branches of the government, stripping the chairman (now called the president) of legislative powers, creating the office of speaker of the council. The tribal council is now clearly the legislative branch, the president heads the executive branch, and the judiciary has firmly established its independence of both. A Navajo Nation has emerged, a nation within the greater nation called the United States. Even so, it is still a "dependent nation" in the terms that Chief Justice John Marshall described Indian tribes almost two centuries ago, and also in the highly pragmatic terms of requiring the assistance of the federal government, which it is due by treaty. But it is a dependent nation with increasing sovereignty over its own affairs and resources and an ever-increasing capacity to deal on an equal basis with the forces of the modern world.

The Navajo Nation is faced, as is any largely rural, undeveloped nation (and even many developed ones), with a host of what seem intractable problems – poverty, unemployment, alcoholism – as well as the added one of maintaining the core of traditional Navajo culture. The challenge is to preserve the particular world-view of the Dineh while taking up what is practical and comfortable from an altogether different and fast-changing outside world. But the Navajos have powerful resources to bring to bear on these problems and challenges, chief among them their own people, now almost a quarter of a million, a people with a long history of adapting to new situations, even the most painful situations, and coming out ahead.

In 1991, President Petersen Zah was inaugurated in front of a crowd of thousands in the Navajo Fair Grounds at Window Rock. As they looked to the future, the various speakers all called upon the great moments in the Navajo past, upon the historic resiliency of the People. A new government was soon at work. One of its members, Rodger Boyd, who trained as an architect and received a degree in regional planning from MIT, and who was appointed by President Zah as director of economic development for the tribe, had earlier said to me and Susanne, "Sure, we'd like to see a personal computer in every hogan on the reservation. We just want them programmed to think Navajo."

Living and learning

Once they were taken on from the Spanish, sheep became the economic mainstay of Navajo culture and a focus of family life. Even small children "own" a sheep or two, which instills in them a sense of individual responsibility within the overall context of communal bonds. At right, near Cottonwood, Arizona, a sheep receives a special treat.

Navajos like to demonstrate that Indians make good cowboys. Those who raise cattle turn lonely herding duties into family affairs when it comes to branding time.

The trick in milking a goat is to keep it
from kicking over the bucket, which this one
subsequently did. But nothing is wasted when
a sheep is butchered for use in a ceremony.

Navajos have also made rodeo their own, with events for men, women (barrel-racing, right), and kids (the woolly riders).

In the calm between rodeo events, seasoned cowboys palaver about their chances and tinker with their gear. Following pages: even nonriders at a rodeo have a chance to compete in a tug-of-war or other games.

Powwows are nontraditional events that Navajos have adopted with enthusiasm. Such music and dance celebrations originated among the Plains Indians and have become occasions that elevate elaborate costumes into an eclectic and ebullient art.

Patriotism runs high at any Navajo country fair or rodeo, and the first to be honored are the veterans of American wars. Princesses, representing tribal government chapters and other local organizations, are chosen for their facility in the traditional tasks of the Navajo matriarch.

Education takes a high priority at Navajo. The students above and below have been encouraged to stay in school through the sponsorship of Albuquerque-based Futures for Children, a program devoted to Indian education and community development.

Surveyor (above), lawyer (far right), and dragline operator are among the many jobs and professions increasingly held by Navajos. Businesses run by the tribal government and by individuals on the reservation have increased, but many people are forced to leave to find work.

Ceremony

Snow made the familiar landscape shrink and tamed the wild shapes, the hard edges, of rock and desert along the road that runs north from Ganado to Chinle through Beautiful Valley. Except for the sprinkling of shrubs and piñons and the occasional dark outcrop of mudstone, its red surface now turned brown, the world was white, horizonless. Sky and earth were one – a monochrome that was both drab and spectacular. It was the time of year when many things can be openly discussed, such things as bears and badgers, lightning, and old stories of origins, without fear that these features of nature (in the form of their Holy People) will turn on you. It was a time when spiders as well are not present so people can play string games – endless variations of what Anglos call cat's cradle.

A Navajo taboo, of which there are many – children learn them like a catechism – says that you don't play string games in the summer because it will cause bad weather, bad luck, and, furthermore, Spider Woman will tie your eyes shut. It was also the season for the Shoe Game, which can only be played at night lest there be a bad snowstorm. The Shoe Game was invented, some say, by Coyote back in the time before there was night and day and the world may well have been as muffled and indistinct a place as it seemed on this mid-January afternoon between snowfalls.

Susanne and I had been invited to join a handful of Anglos and attend a Shoe Game in Pinon, about sixty miles west of Chinle in the approximate middle of Black Mesa. By the time we reached Pinon, our first visit in several years, the sky had cleared and a thin wintry sun made the snow dazzle. It was warm enough to turn the town's dirt roads into slippery mud. There was a new school in addition to the old boarding school and about twenty new frame houses on the edge of town, all in one stage or another of construction and being built, we later learned, to house Navajos who had to be relocated out of what was no longer Joint Use Land. At the trading post we met up with the other invitees, six people from Taos, New Mexico, two of whom were long-standing friends of the Navajo family hosting the Shoe Game.

Before long, in a caravan of four-wheel-drive vehicles, we were sliding and bucking along a dirt track that was now a river of mud and slush, leading after a mile or so to a camp that consisted mostly of a frame house and an extra-large hogan. We were greeted by several enthusiastic dogs, a few standoffish chickens, and Valencia Begay, who invited us into her mother's kitchen to eat dinner – fry bread, a chili and mutton stew, and blue corn bread with raisins, neatly wrapped in cornhusks. Meanwhile, someone handed out pieces of string tied into loops, and informal string game lessons proceeded. The simplest pattern is called bird's nest or, alternatively, teacup and saucer, and the Anglos painstakingly and slowly produced this after

Greeting the year's first snow showers with bare chest, and with yells and shrieks, makes a young boy "feel good" and puts his system in balance with nature. Intimate contact with the cycle of the seasons forms a part of every Navajo's life.

In its many versions, the string game provides winter amusement and reflects the patterns found in both the night sky and traditional rugs.

much instruction, while the kids who were present were cranking out astonishing patterns with swift, almost balletic gestures of hand and wrist. A family member told me, "If it wasn't for these string games, we Navajos would go crazy in the wintertime. There's practically nothing to do this time of year with all this snow."

Several years earlier, we had come across string games in an unusual place – a classroom at the Navajo Community College in Tsaile, where a medicine man named Andy Notanabah was teaching a class in Navajo astronomy. Some of the patterns created in string games, he said, represent the seven constellations, those that First Man so conscientiously arranged in the sky – Scorpio, Cassiopeia, the Pleides, Aldabran, Canis Major, Ursa Major, and the belt and sword of Orion. The constellations correspond, as well, to the seven important parts of the human body, Andy said: the arms and hands, the legs and feet, the torso, the head, and the heart. So when a child learns the string games, and the names of the patterns formed, he is also learning about the Navajo sky, among other things. Furthermore, the medicine man said, the string-game patterns that represent the constellations are also geometrically the same as the traditional patterns woven into Navajo rugs.

In any event, unlike First Man, I was too butterfingered to get past the teacup and saucer, and began to harbor thoughts of how foolish I would appear if invited to actually *play* some role in the Shoe Game later that evening. There had been a Shoe Game the night before in the community center in Pinon, heavily attended, and a lot of the same people were excited, we were told, to know of tonight's game "with white people." We were surely being set up, I thought, and while we continued to get our fingers tangled up in string, Valencia stood up and explained some things about Shoe Games.

It began, she said, back when there was no day or night. There were creatures then, ones we now think of as day creatures (like stinkbugs and badgers) and night creatures (like owls), but they were yet to take on their present bodily forms. The world was also gravely threatened by monsters, one of whom was in the habit of eating whatever creatures it ran into. On

112

one occasion, Coyote unwittingly bumped into this monster and realized he was in deep trouble. Instead of running, which would have been no use, Coyote said, "Hello. You're just the one I was looking for. I've invented a game and I want you to play it." And he very quickly racked his brains to invent a game, which was the Shoe Game (sometimes called the Moccasin Game). This ploy by Coyote to save his neck was the first lie in this world.

As it worked out, the game was to be played by two teams, the night creatures and the day creatures, and the outcome would decide if there would be permanent night or permanent day. The unexpected result was that, after playing all night, neither side could win, so there is both day and night now. When dawn approached, it was imperative that all the animals go home, but the birds were allowed to choose whatever bright colors they wanted for themselves. Raven, who had been asleep during all this, woke up to find that there were no colors left except the charcoal from the fire, so he became black. Meanwhile Bear, who had also been asleep (and whose moccasins had been among those used in the game), was in such a rush to leave that he put his moccasins on the wrong feet (the right moccasin on the left foot and vice versa), which is why today the bear's feet are strangely turned. And the tinge of red on a bear's fur is a result of his lateness that (first) day when the Sun glinted red on him.

With its origins described, Valencia explained that the Shoe Game was related to the Beauty Way ceremony, and the songs sung during the game were the same as some of the Beauty Way songs – about how the creatures like stinkbugs and badgers each have their own beauty way. The difference, she said, is that the Shoe Game is not as serious, as formal, as other ceremonies. You can, for example, make jokes about your sisters and brothers. Much of the laughing and jokes are to try to distract the other team. Another difference, of course, is that the Shoe Game is a gambling game. Then she briefly reviewed the rules and said it was time now to go over to the hogan where the game would be played. The two singers (team leaders) and the others would arrive as soon as the ground froze, making it easier to drive up the track.

I for one have no idea exactly how it becomes clear when it is time for a Navajo ceremony to begin, what signal is received by whom, how everything is set in motion. This ceremony appeared to begin more or less of its own accord, the way water curling and roiling out of a faucet suddenly becomes a steady stream. Susanne and I had gone over to the hogan with the others, finding a large packed-earth floor, with benches and sofas ranged around the walls, and a simple woodstove made from an oil drum with a pipe that rose through the ceiling. In the northern sector, on the floor, was a pile of loose sandy soil, matched by a corresponding pile in the southern sector. People began to drift in, bringing drafts of icy air with them – men, women, young people of both sexes, infants, old grandmothers. A pair of brawny men with humorous eyes came in and began talking to Susanne and me. One, a fellow named Ray wearing a Washington Redskins hat, explained that yes, he was a Redskins fan, that he was going to cheer his team to the Superbowl, and began to tell me about the rules of the Shoe Game. Meanwhile, the other of the two, wearing a straw cowboy hat and a gray sweatshirt, and who we learned was named Harold Begay, took Susanne through some of the more sophisticated string games. A number of people were doing string games around the hogan, some of them competing to see who could do a pattern the fastest, leading to some dazzling displays of adroitness that looked like intense conversations using the sign language of the deaf.

Ray explained that there were four shoes buried under each pile of earth, that one team would hide a ball in one of their shoes, fill them all up with sand, and the other team had to guess which shoe the ball was in. If the other team got it right, they got the ball. This much I already knew from Valencia's description, and I also knew that the score was kept by the use of a bundle of 102 strips of yucca. Valencia had said that they represented the number of years of a long life (100) with two extra-long strips in addition "to play with." But how the scoring was done remained a mystery. In the hogan, Ray said there was a lot of intuition involved, and that if anyone on the team thought he or she could help, they should speak up.

The scoring, Ray said, was similar to volleyball. When you have the ball and are hiding it, it's like serving: the only time you can score points. And you score points from your opponents' errors. For example, when a member of the other team approaches your pile of sand, he has two choices. He can say that the ball is *not* in this particular shoe. If it *is* in that shoe, he loses ten points for his team, and ten of the yucca strips are given to his opponents. Or if the ball is not in the shoe, he may proceed, specifying yet another shoe where the ball *isn't*, with the same penalty for being wrong. Or he can, at any time, specify a shoe where he thinks the ball actually is hidden. If he is wrong, he again loses points – six if he is far off, four if he is off by one shoe. If he is right, he and his team get the ball and can begin scoring points. The team that winds up with all the yucca strips wins the game.

Meanwhile, a rather severe-looking young man stood up amidst the milling crowd – by now about fifty people – and held up a small disk of what looked like cornhusk. One side was black, the other light, and he made a great point of showing both sides to anyone who was looking. I gathered that he was one of the singers and that we were about to see some equivalent of a coin toss. He then took out a black bandanna and began waving it in the air, shaking it out like a blanket, finally tossing it over on the pile of sand on what was my side of the hogan. Still, people were milling around, talking, playing string games. Then suddenly an older man in a red shirt and red peaked cap was standing in the middle of the hogan, talking loudly in Navajo, and everyone stopped talking. When he was done, there was a sudden bustle of activity, with Susanne's string game mentor, Harold Begay, accepting dollar bills and laying them out carefully on the black bandanna. Ray told me that only bettors could participate, so, with some misgivings, I put in $3. Valencia came over to explain that the medicine man in the red shirt had said, among other things, that since the Shoe Game involved summer animals, it could only be played in the winter. She also said that he felt that the game should not be photographed since the photographs might be looked at during the wrong period of the year and that would get him – and the other singer (who was our Harold Begay) – in trouble with the Holy People of the summer animals.

Harold counted the bets: $42. Then he went over to the other team, who had counted their bets: $45. Harold called out these numbers and a member of our team provided another $3 to equalize the bets. All the money was wrapped up in the black bandanna, which was placed on a windowsill beside an eagle feather. I was unaware of any particular choosing up of sides, by the way. One seemed to be on a given team simply by virtue of where one happened to be when the game began, but I suspect that there was some form of selection. At any rate, it turned out that the red-shirted singer was a serious man and his team serious about winning, while Harold Begay seemed jollier about the whole thing; our team was a bit more loose, even raucous. Our team lost the cornhusk toss, so two members of the other team – the north, or night animal, team – held up a blanket between us and their pile of sand. When it was lowered, Harold crossed the hogan, picked up a smooth, barkless stick, and knelt before the pile of earth. He scraped away the sand from the tops of the moccasins while the red-shirted singer loudly chanted a song, joined by a few others. Harold then banged on the shoe tops with the stick, finally reaching into one, digging it out, and coming up empty-handed, to the loud guffaws and cheers from the night team. "Six," they shouted, "six." And a kid holding the bundle of yucca strips took six and handed them to the night people. Harold retired, grinning broadly, and the blanket was raised again.

I was told that if you bang on a shoetop with the stick two or more times, you are in effect saying that you don't believe the ball is in that shoe. If you hit a shoetop one blow, you are saying that's where the ball is. Some people would approach the shoes and bang repeatedly, heads cocked, as if listening, while others used the stick more perfunctorily. Matters of style.

Eventually, one of our day people got it right and brought the ball to our side. This highly prized object looked like a small brown egg, or a nut, and I was told it was from the inside of a yucca plant. Our blanket was raised, the ball elaborately hidden, and sand heaped up over the shoes. As a night team member approached, Harold broke into a loud and ebullient song, soon joined by some other men sitting on benches by the wall. I suspected that Harold was working some variations on these traditional songs – typically about stinkbugs or badgers or whatever – since people tended to burst out laughing in the middle of them. He was evidently trying to break the concentration of the other side, and this would become all the more pronounced when his opposite number, the night team's singer in the red shirt, approached. The songs were then louder, and most of the men on our side would huddle around, singing, peering closely, crowding him. And when the night singer missed, there was loud and prolonged joy in dayville. It seemed fairly clear that, among all the meanings and functions of the Shoe Game, it was something of a test of strength between the two singers, who are also medicine men.

As the night wore on, the fire in the stove dwindled but the heat of what was by now sixty-odd humans was ample. Periodically, Valencia and others of her family would pass coffee, cakes, apples, and such among the people; infants cried, suckled, and slept; some old grandmothers dozed on the benches; string-game patterns would emerge from the crowd; and the raucous singing and shouting reverberated in the hogan, as the ball changed hands and teams cheered or fell silent depending on the momentary fortunes of the game. The day people won the first game, each member being paid twice what he or she had bet, and after a bit of fresh air in the bitter cold outside, a new game began. In all, we played five games, the last ending at three o'clock in the morning. After a game was won, and before the money was passed out, Harold would take all the yucca strips and go over to one or another of the old ladies sitting against the wall and touch her in various places with the yucca, emitting loud whoops that sounded to me like "Ho!" We were told that this was to help heal an ailment the lady was suffering. The day people won all but the third game, and if there were any sour grapes on the part of the night team it was not evident.

Typically, there was no effort to designate who should pick up the stick and represent his or her team. Someone – sometimes after a long pause – would simply get up and take the stick. Occasionally, one or another of the regulars would call out for some person to take the stick and, in the course of the first two games, Harold held the stick out to me three times. My first attempt produced a loss of ten points, the second produced the ball for our side, and the third try netted a loss of four. When I was wrong the first time, my opponents pointed to the proper shoetop and I nodded, getting up to leave. But they told me I should dig it up and see that they were telling the truth.

(Evidently, in the first Shoe Game, Owl introduced cheating to the world, pretending to hide the ball in the moccasin of the night team but instead keeping it hidden in his hand. The other team sent some gophers down underground to check and they found that the ball was in none of the moccasins. It was eventually found in Owl's possession and the situation was brought back to normal. In the meantime, however, the holes that had to be made in the soles of the moccasins to uncover the ruse led to the new fact of life that moccasins would all eventually wear out and have to be replaced, thus providing additional work for Navajos, and with the salutary effect of keeping idle hands busy. In our Shoe Game, moccasins had been replaced by what I took to be low-ankled workboots.)

At various times, people would get on a hot streak. Harold found the ball about four times in a row, and a young Navajo woman on our side had a long streak where she simply would walk up to the shoes, bend over, and extract the ball without any fanfare or stickwork whatsoever. In any event, hot streaks and dry spells aside, there was clearly a lot of attempted intuition involved, not just random guesswork. A kid on the night team, maybe eight years old and named Arsenio, seemed to be preternaturally accurate, and his name was heard often above the hubbub. As it turned out, so was mine.

Part of the way into the third game (the first two having taken well over two hours), Susanne and I were seated on a bench against the wall when she told me that she seemed to be able to sense which shoe the ball had been put in. There have been many times in her life when she has found herself sensing things that are beyond what can be determined by the physical senses (sight, hearing, etc.), so this did not astonish me. And in due course, when Harold held the stick out to me, I asked Susanne which shoe. She said "East." So I approached the pile of earth, pushed the sand away from the tops, and tapped twice on the west shoe and the one next to it, while a man from the night team was kneeling next to me, shoving a little, singing loudly in my ear and grinning like a wolf. Then I tapped once on the easternmost shoe, dug the sand out, and there was the ball, which I flipped to Harold.

A while later I was handed the stick again and turned to Susanne; she once more said "East." And again, I got the ball back for our team. Over the next half hour or so, I got the ball back twice more without a miss and, by the beginning of the fourth game, my team was looking at me in an odd if approving way, while the other team was saying things like "Here comes that guy again." At one point, Susanne said she was tired (it was by then about one o'clock in the morning), and when my team called out my name and held the stick out, Susanne reluctantly named a shoe and I missed. But she got a second wind, and I retrieved the ball for the day people five more times, in all nine out of ten under Susanne's guidance. The night team's singer, the old fellow in the red shirt, would regard me each time that I approached with a not completely friendly wariness. The young Navajo woman on our team, who had had her own hot streak, eventually realized that it was Susanne doing my sensing and, on two occasions, asked her which shoe to tap and got it right both times. In all, when asked, Susanne got it right eleven out of twelve times, remarkable even (evidently) in a Shoe Game.

When the fifth game was over, people milled around and drifted into the night, where some twenty pickup engines roared in the frigid air. Ray said good-bye and we agreed that the Redskins were unquestionably the team to beat (the next day, with Ray's support, they beat Detroit to qualify for the Superbowl, which they went on to win). Harold came up and shook hands with us, asking me how I did it. I said, "Susanne would tell me. She could sense where they'd put it."

Harold smiled happily. "Yeah, I could see her thinking over there. I thought so." Then he went on to say that his technique was different. When the other team was hiding the ball, he would concentrate "real hard" and try to influence the placement of the ball, in a sense causing them to put the ball in the shoe he (Harold) had in mind. And we were struck by an extraordinary difference between Navajo and Anglo. For a Navajo, thinking is a directly creative act, a way to intervene actively and affect the outcome of events in the Navajo world, beyond what we typically see as physical causes and effects. It is in this manner that the medicine man heals. (On hearing about our game-playing later, a Navajo friend suggested that the night team would have been exerting itself to block us, but would have been unable to since we weren't Navajo and Susanne was playing, in a sense, a different game.)

As Harold headed off into the icy night, he said, "All you need now as Shoe Game players is to learn the songs." I thought to myself that I would do that. My pronunciation would be so bad that all the words would mean something else (probably ribald) and the other team would be distracted.

We slept in bedrolls on the dirt floor of the hogan along with the other Anglo guests and, while my dreams are typically not specific to recent events, the Shoe Game continued in my head until dawn. It had been a game, a gambling game, one I thought might easily engage the gambling folk (or addicts) who now flock to so many Indian reservations where – I like to think – by way of getting even for the European introduction of hard booze, a number of tribes happily take *our* addicts' money in Bingo and other gambling games. I thought also of the august and solemn chants of the Episcopal church, reverberating with high pomp in vast, echoing naves of gray stone, services I had once, long ago, been forced to attend twice daily as a schoolboy. I recalled the explanations of humanity's sinful nature, and the oleaginous (and astoundingly sexist) directions to the redemptive path available to good Roman Catholic Pueblo Indian couples being wed in old missions by modern Franciscans along the Rio Grande. And I dwelled on the wondrous grin on Harold Begay's face when he, or I, or someone else, brought back the ball, and I thought: That's my kind of ceremony. Because, with all the good fun, that is what it had been, this Shoe Game, a ceremony: where old ladies had been amused, honored, and perhaps healed; where sixty people, some of them strangers to one another, had communed in raucous cheering and, as silly as it sounds, team spirit – all in direct kinship with some notions set forth by the Holy People in times unimaginably long past and still present. The Navajo world had again been set right, and *I* knew that. So had my world, and that doesn't happen every day.

A Navajo medicine man recently said that there is no way to explain the Navajo religion to people who don't speak Navajo in all its verbal richness. This is not an uncommon thought, not only among Navajo people, but any with a different language and view of the world. The nuances, presumably, are beyond alien comprehension. One taps on such doors quietly and nervously, awaiting a quiet face behind the screen, a face that is not likely to be loquacious.

But some Navajos have been forthcoming over the generations about these supremely private matters, and from time to time have even let aliens sit in on some of their ceremonies. They are mostly healing ceremonies, events in which the balance of things is put right, cosmic chiropractic where the spine of the world is kneaded by story and prayer back into alignment so that some individual, who has organized the ceremony for himself or herself, may again be well. Some ceremonies take as many as nine days. The Navajo medicine man doesn't do these things for nothing. A major ceremony may cost thousands of dollars by today's kind of reckoning, much of it cash – not just blankets and other barter. The medicine man must know all the chants by heart, he must repeat them *perfectly*, lest something awful slip through the crack of error and make it not just not work but the reverse – make matters worse. In such ceremonies, the "patient" is in the hands of the medicine man or medicine woman, and the doctor is somewhere out there negotiating with the wayward moods and awesome power of the Holy People. It takes a certain courage, and a lot of the right kind of persuasion. And the chants, of course, were laid out long ago as part of the story of Navajo becoming; where one heard them, from what clan, what region, what mentor, makes a big difference. But, once learned, they must be iterated *perfectly* or they don't work.

It is all utterly logical, if you believe that there are countervailing forces at large, some with a kind of benign, easygoing temperament, which like to see things going harmoniously, and others which cannot resist interfering and making things cacophonous, unbalanced – meddlers, that section of the orchestra that simply has to mess up the symphony of life.

When he was a young man, Billy Yellow was in the movies. He was an extra in a film starring John Wayne, stirringly shot in Monument Valley, the place which, thanks to oaters and auto ads, some people think is what the whole Southwest looks like. When Susanne and I met him, a half-century after his film career, he was a vigorous eighty-five-year-old with a ready smile seaming a face that even at rest looked like canyon country. He lived in his wife's camp west of Monument Valley, but not so far west that the tops of some of that Navajo tribal park's cathedrallike buttes are obscured. The camp consisted of a house, a couple of shadehouses (wooden frames covered with branches), a few outbuildings, horse and sheep corrals, and a traditional hogan made of logs and covered with mud. All around, red sand and desert scrub stretched away, reaching up to the east to some low red cliffs that turn vermillion in the setting sun: a place of surpassing beauty, and of a silence as great as the sky overhead.

Susanne had signed on with a Canadian film crew, shooting a segment of the public television series called *Millennium*, and Billy Yellow had agreed to something extremely rare, perhaps unheard of. A medicine man, he had agreed to let the crew film a healing ceremony, specifically a Red Antway ceremony that Billy was going to conduct for one of his young grandsons. The boy had a chronic skin problem because, it was said, two years earlier his father had inadvertently killed a snake. Billy Yellow is not a shy man, and, of course, he had already had experience before the cameras, but he was taking this unprecedented step, he said, because he thought it would be useful for other people in the world to see such a ceremony, so that they might learn to respect such things. His father, Billy explained, had told him that times were changing, that Navajo medicine men should feel obliged to heal anyone, not just Navajo people.

Most such healing ceremonies take place at night or in the morning or both, but this ceremony's main events – chanting or singing over the boy while he sat on a sand painting on two successive days – took place in the afternoon. That simply may be the way Billy Yellow does the Red Antway ceremony. Anthropologist Leland C. Weyman, in a book on this ceremony, describes some twenty separate rites running from sundown through the night into forenoon, and lasting up to nine days, but with many variations from one place to another, one medicine man or singer (*hataatsi*) to another.

Incidental to the preparations for the ceremony was a twenty-minute drive to an Anglo friend's house on the rim of the small canyon in Medicine Hat, Utah, through which the San Juan River runs. Here Billy and his son-in-law sat chatting with two Anglo friends in the late afternoon at a picnic table, while hummingbirds whirred around a feeding station hung on the side of the house. Eventually, Billy approached the feeding station and wrapped a red cloth halfway around it. When a hummingbird approached he would quickly snap the cloth the rest of the way around and, after a couple of aborted attempts, he reached into the cloth and, however improbable it seems to anyone who knows how fast hummingbirds can move, came out with one cupped in his large brown hand. He called a different grandson over (one he was grooming to be a medicine man one day) and proceeded to touch him with the hummingbird, starting at the feet and proceeding to his head, enjoining him in all his movements, all his travels, to fly like the hummingbird. Thought creates the plan of the world, speech brings it about, and motion is life: motion should be beautiful, like that of the hummingbird.

Among the preparations, the old man had spent hours out in the surrounding desert with the "patient," talking, explaining the old stories. On the days of the ceremony, the two, along with two of the boy's age mates, spent time in a sweat lodge, singing. In another act of purification, Billy dug up a large chunk of yucca root, made shampoo from it, and washed his long gray hair.

About midmorning, Billy and his son-in-law went into the hogan and began to create a sandpainting on the sandy floor. From a purely practical standpoint, it seems uncanny that so precise and elaborate a creation can arise from a thin trickle of colored sand from between a thumb and forefinger – straight lines, perfect arcs – symbolically depicting events, meanings, and Holy People. This has been called the Navajo's highest art form and, from a Western aesthetic standpoint, it seems bewildering that after the ceremony, so grand a work is destroyed, the colored lines scuffed into the underlying sand, scooped up, and taken away. The sand is taken out to the east, lest it cause evil, and one doesn't shake out the blanket of sand lest it cause a windstorm and scatter the absorbed evil. This is, of course, sacred art, a notion much attenuated in Western civilization, and for Navajo the "art" is in the act of creation, and in what the sandpainting will accomplish. After that, it is of no value; indeed, it is what we might think of as toxic. (There are some traditional medicine men and others who are made uneasy by the production and sale of smaller versions of sandpaintings, made permanent by mixing sand and glue, just as there are those still who are uneasy about some Navajo weavers introducing ceremonial symbols into their rugs.)

A purpose of the sandpainting, as well as much of the rest of the ceremony, is – as Billy Yellow explained it – to bring the timeless people together with the people of time. The Holy People and the Earth-Surface People. The Holy People – for example, the Ant People – are taken to be largely indifferent to humans, but if a human does something wrong, such as inadvertently eating an ant, or walking on or urinating on an anthill, the Ant People are offended and can visit upon the wrongdoer a great deal of trouble – abdominal ills, rashes, sore throats, ominous dreams, rheumatism, and so forth. Since horned toads feed on ants and are believed to be impervious to injury from lightning and thunder, they, along with thunder and lightning, can be invoked to relieve the problems caused by the Ant People – as, of course, can the Ant People themselves.

Once the sandpainting was complete in Billy Yellow's hogan and the family and visitors were fed, everyone assembled, the boy was placed, sitting, on the sandpainting and Billy took up a rattle and began to sing. At one point, he held out a saucer from which the boy drank some (evidently foultasting) herbal medicine. After about an hour of chanting, occasionally joined by his wife, he ceased, approached the boy, and touched him here and there with jerky thrusts of a piece of paraphernalia, emitting abrupt squeaks with each touch. And the ceremony was over. The sandpainting was scuffed into oblivion, the sand collected in a blanket, and Billy's son-in-law took it out of the hogan. The Holy People had been enticed to come, to enter the sandpainting and, from there, the boy. They had been obligated, by the law of reciprocity, to set things right. And with the remnants of the painting taken out of the hogan, they could leave.

Given the complexity and demands of any given ceremony (imagine knowing the precise wording of the songs that will take up a good part of nine days), a medicine man or woman will be a practitioner of maybe just one, but rarely more than a few particular "sings." In trying to make some kind of taxonomic order out of all these ceremonies, Western anthropologists have tried out various schemes but are the first to confess that the Navajo language has no word that is a counterpart to the English word religion. Indeed, some have suggested that each ceremony, such as the Red Antway, constitutes a distinct religion of its own, and Navajos, in proper season and given the exigencies of the moment, are aided by some fifty such religions that can be brought into action as needed. But there does seem to be some order to all this.

Billy Yellow's Red Antway ceremony falls into what might be thought of as a ceremonial category called a Holyway, and there are as many as twenty-four different Holyway ceremonies – each one of which serves to heal a different, though sometimes overlapping, range of ills arising from some act or attitude that has created an unbalance or disharmony that in turn brings down the wrath of some group of Holy People. While these ceremonies may last nine days (computed from the beginning of a night to the beginning of the next), there are usually five-day and two-day forms as well. But there are other kinds of ceremonies. One is the Blessingway, of which there are several minor variants. This is not a healing rite. Instead, it calls forth blessings for good luck, for protection of people and their things. It can protect one's sheep, bless a new house or ceremonial materials, help ease childbirth, bring rain and good crops. It may be sung for soldiers or new tribal officials or at weddings; the female puberty ceremony *kinaalda* is a version of the Blessingway. According to Leland Wyman, Navajos "regard Blessingway as the backbone of their religion and give it historical precedence over all other ceremonies." A standard feature of Blessingway is the use of pollen, usually corn pollen, which symbolizes happiness and fertility. Everything needing to be blessed gets a pinch of pollen. One prays by taking some from a pouch, putting some in one's mouth, some on top of one's head, and tossing the rest out in front. This simple pollen prayer is how many Navajos, standing outside the entrance of their hogans or houses, greet the dawn, or express their gratitude for a good dream.

There is a different category of healing ceremonies. These are called Evilways or Ghostways and many of them are versions of the Holyways – such as the Red Antway – and are directed at healing much the same ills as their Holyway counterparts. But in this case, the ills arise from other sources: notably, contact with the ghost of someone departed, or from witchcraft. While Holyway chants may both invoke the presence of Holy People *and*

Corn pollen, used in ceremonies, prayers, and private blessings, is shaken from the tassels into a basket.

have elements of exorcism, the Evilway chants are almost completely given over to exorcisms.

Individual rituals within an Evilway ceremony may include having the patient, the "one sung over," enter the hogan through several large hoops made of branches, over a trail made of sandpainting. As the afflicted, wearing a cloth over his head, moves along the trail through the hoops, the singer gradually removes the cloth, returning things to normal. A variant of this is that structures, ceremonially made from yucca strips or evergreen boughs, may be wrapped around the seated patient. In the course of the ceremony, men impersonating the Slayer Twins, who freed the world of monsters, cut these plants up and take them away, freeing the patient of the disease.

One of these ceremonies, the Enemyway, is directed against alien ghosts, particularly those encountered by warriors in the course of battle. The Enemyway ceremony was widely practiced on behalf of veterans returning from action in Vietnam and, more recently, Desert Storm. But others than warriors may require the ceremony. In a world that contains both *hozho* and its opposite, both good and evil, even the best of men and women may leave behind an angry, vengeful ghost. If the person was not buried properly, or if its grave is disturbed, and for other reasons, such as avenging a slur made during the person's lifetime, the ghost can cause various kinds of sickness. One does not willingly mention the name of a dead relative lest its ghost be attracted. (Similarly, one does not discuss such things as bears except during winter when they are hibernating.) Indeed, a host of taboos surround the dead. One shouldn't cut one's hair for four days after a death, sleep with the head toward the north or toward the head end of a sheepskin, shake out one's bedding at night, look into a mirror or wash one's hair at night: all such acts invoke ghosts.

While a good deal of most ceremonies takes place at night, night is generally considered not a good time to be abroad, for this is the time when the witches prowl, and witchcraft is almost universally dreaded among the Navajo. Great care is taken about such personal things as nail clippings, hair, feces, and even the use of one's real Navajo name, lest they fall into the hands of a witch who can use them as "the one sung over" in the malevolent misuse of rituals to cause one harm. One is careful about shaking hands with strangers, even talking about a stranger, since he or she might be a witch. One never sleeps with feet away from the door, or wears a ring on the thumb or forefinger, since that is what witches do. Even a bare footprint or a handprint in the snow can be used by a witch.

In some instances, medicine men, already steeped in ritual knowledge, are suspected of being witches, but that is evidently a society open to anyone of an evil mind. A friend told Susanne that one becomes a witch by, among other things, committing certain unspeakable acts – murdering a kinsman, incest. In the seventies, she visited a man widely reputed to be a witch, who openly confessed to having had a child by his daughter.

Witches are said to have certain supernatural powers, such as the ability to take the form of an upright wolf and to run along beside the fastest pickup. These are the "skin walkers." Certain stretches of road, such as the Summit – that part of Route 264 that begins rising at St. Michaels, passes through forested land, and descends to Ganado – have a reputation for being especially subject to these apparitions during the night. There are some people who deplore many of the changes of modernity among Indian people, for example, the great rows of stanchions for high-tension wires that are now seen virtually everywhere across the Navajo landscape. One of the many benefits, however, is that many remote Navajo camps now have a single street lamp that casts a large circle of light over their dwellings in the fastness and fearfulness of night. Modernity, in the form of electricity, does not necessarily alter the ancient order of beliefs.

If one fears having been witched, or is suffering from what is deemed to be witchcraft, one or another of the Ghostway ceremonies must be done as a healing. Sometimes even more is done. A diviner may be consulted who may succeed in identifying the witch; then another ceremony is performed. It is a version of the Enemyway, also called a Squaw Dance because, during the evening, young women get to choose their partners in the dancing that takes place around a vast fire in the center of a circle of pickups and cars. But earlier, before dark, some twenty or so men on horseback appear ominously on the horizon, riding toward the camp. They thunder at full gallop into camp. One of them holds a pouch in front of him, which is immediately taken into a hogan. And, it is said, the witch (some of whose hair or some other personal effect is in the pouch) has exactly a year before he or she will be dead of some violent and often inexplicable cause. The man whom Susanne visited was later found dead. He was discovered one morning crushed in his pickup, with its front-end smashed in, on a flat and featureless stretch of desert near a straight, flat road. There were no signs in the desert or on the road of the presence of any other vehicle.

Accompanied by his supporters, a man needing a special kind of healing rides across the horizon toward a Squaw Dance.

In a program funded by the National Institute of Mental Health in the late 1960s, new medicine people were given training. The notebook shows special symbols one student used to keep track of the order of a ceremony. Below is a tray holding a medicine man's ceremonial objects for a Beautyway ceremony.

Of course there is more to Navajo ceremony than this. The Blessingway ceremony, or some segment of it, may be brought to bear at the end of any other ceremony for what might be thought of as an insurance policy, in case some error may have crept into the chant. Perhaps more (or less) analogous, it is like a spelling check program on a computer. Errors or omissions are weeded out, so that a flawed ceremony is not rendered ineffectual or dangerous. If this precautionary device sounds close to what we might, laically, call a tool, it is not improper to think of much of the medicine man's work as the use of tools.

On one occasion, at a workshop hosted at the Navajo Community College for medicine men and Indian Service doctors, there was a marvelous session in which Navajo medicine men opened their bundles, called *jish*, to the inspection of the doctors, who in turn opened their bags of stethoscopes and other equipment. The two groups peered at these utensils with fascination, though perhaps not total comprehension. The contents of a doctor's black bag are, after all, simply tools – inert, mechanical, or chemical. The contents of a medicine man's pouch are sacred and alive – *jish* refers not only to the pouch but to the contents. A book of more than six hundred pages has been written about these pouches, their contents, use, and the methods by which they can be passed along, or not. Documented also are other sacred ceremonial paraphernalia, each item of which is typically collected painstakingly and individually blessed. Suffice it to say that a medicine man may need to possess a toolkit that includes, to quote from that book, "herbs, rattles, fetishes, small pottery bowls, whistles, shells, feathers, bullroarers, unraveling cords, arrowheads, miniature bows and arrows, reeds, small pieces of buckskin, small individual pouches of sacred pollen and medicines, and paint pigments."

Attempts to categorize or quantify so kaleidoscopic and individualistic a system are difficult. It may be thought of as religion, but it is also a medical system. And it operates among a people so numerous and so widespread, with so many local traditions, that efforts to define it probably will continue to defy the cataloguing of science and probably will continue to defy even total comprehension by every Navajo. One can consult the books, one can consult the range of Navajo acquaintances, to get a feel for this sort of thing, to sense and maybe illuminate the spirit of this multifarious enterprise. Or relate an anecdote.

Several years ago, Susanne became aware that many Navajo medicine men required quartz crystals for some of their diagnostic techniques. Some people who diagnose illnesses at Navajo use a technique called hand-trembling: they go into a trancelike state and, as their hands tremble involuntarily, they are able to see the locus of a sickness (say, the kidneys) and also its cause. Thus can the proper healing ceremony be specified, the appropriate singer selected. Other diagnosticians use crystals, peering at the afflicted through one (or a pair) to see the source of trouble. Stargazing is yet another diagnostic system, amplifying through a crystal the meaning of the stars and constellations.

In any event, given the laws of reciprocity, it seemed a good idea to bring quartz crystals to the Navajo when we visited, so Susanne started a crystal-importing business in our home, then in Virginia, the proceeds of which would provide her with a personal collection and a supply for those Navajo acquaintances who could use them. Among her crystals was a large, clear one that we bought in Brazil that she carried with her always. It seemed to have a feeling to it of well-being. Then a medicine man who had befriended us took us to a *Yei-be-chei* ceremony, one of the Holyway ceremonies when masked impersonators of the Holy People, called *yeis*, appear, typically at the end of a several-day-long ceremony. In this instance, we drove the medicine man to a Navajo camp off the road leading north out of Tsaile. We pulled up among about a dozen pickups outside a large hogan with a dirt roof. To the east, the Lukachukai mountains rose up jaggedly. The medicine man told us to stay put, which we did while he went inside. About fifteen minutes later, he emerged and waved us in. Inside, another medicine man and what we were told were two "professional" sandpainters were completing the last of a dozen stylized *yeis* in a sandpainting that spread about sixteen feet across the hogan's dirt floor. The men worked on their knees with amazing speed and dexterity, picking each color of sand from its own plastic dish. After watching this for a few minutes, we were told to run an errand. When we came back from the Tsaile trading post with a large supply of apples to hand out, countless pickups had pulled up in a circle, forming a kind of plaza outside the hogan where two bonfires had been started. For some forty minutes, we waited in the cool breeze and warm sun while some people strode purposefully back and forth and others simply lolled around. Presently, two figures in feathered headdresses and wearing blankets emerged from the hogan and made their way to a shack at the north end of the open space. In due course, three *yeis* emerged from the shack, dancing. They hooted at each other, moving back and forth; several women in blankets approached them and sprinkled cornmeal. Then, as abruptly as it had begun, it was over; the dancers returned to the hogan. Two women we had met introduced us to the man whose wife the ceremony had been given for, and Susanne offered him some apples. In turn, he invited us to come to the shade house for a meal of coffee, fry bread, and mutton stew with carrots and celery.

During the course of the meal, our medicine man friend got a glimpse of Susanne's Brazilian crystal and said, "Give it to me." Her reaction was to say no. Her next reaction was not to incur the disfavor of the medicine man. Her third reaction was to remind herself that the man had been coughing all day and was certainly exhausted, if not ill, from his endless round of duties and that he might be able to make some helpful use of the crystal that lay beyond what it could do for Susanne. She relinquished it, and drove back to Gallup that day in silence. He told us later that he had fixed the crystal over the doorway to his own house, a protection for himself and his family as he continued his parlous negotiations with the moody Holy People, trying to set things right in a world that contains both good and evil.

Near Monument Valley, medicine man Billy Yellow prays to a yucca plant before removing a chunk of its root, which he will make into a purifying shampoo prior to his performing a healing "sing."

Billy Yellow and the patient, his grandson, purify themselves in a sweatlodge. At right and below are Billy's *jish* – the ceremonial objects needed for a Red Antway ceremony. Susanne was permitted to photograph this ceremony because Billy Yellow decided the outside world should see it, so that others might learn respect for Navajo healing.

For each day of a Red Antway ceremony, a new sandpainting is created, using natural pigments that are ground into powder and laid down with painstaking care. When complete, the sandpainting is considered to be "alive."

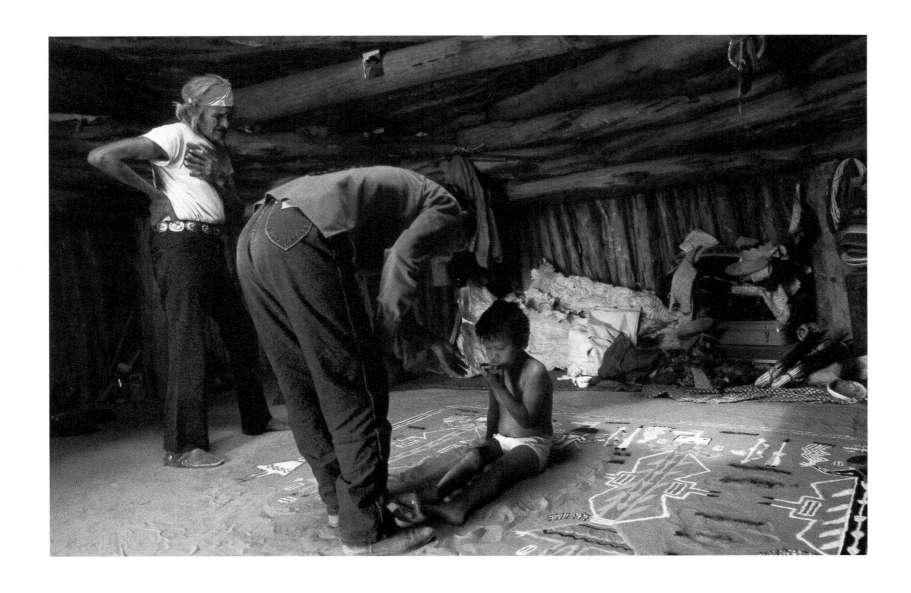

During the ceremony, the boy's father gives him a bitter herbal drink, while the medicine man, his grandfather, sings to the accompaniment of a rattle. Once the world is put right and the sandpainting is destroyed and taken away, life can go on in harmony.

Crystal

Crystal, New Mexico, can be reached in three ways by road and each of them can be a challenge, given the unpredictable nature of most Navajo dirt roads off the highway, especially in winter. On a typical day in winter, snow from the night before has given way to the sun and a perfectly sound four-wheel-drive vehicle will sink into a morass of mud above its axle, all four wheels whirring deeper into the earth.

Crystal is what a map says is a town, a proper dot with a road running through it, but it is really a Navajo encampment, a series of encampments, a prosperous-looking agricultural place that would make the Swiss purse their lips with approval. There are well-fenced green fields in season, trim demarcations of areas bespeaking ancient agreements. There are clearly marked municipal buildings and, on the edges, a healthy forest that rises up like a cloak on the mountainsides – piñon pines that in season drip with nuts – and pasturelands, and organized realms for corn plants, tidy herds of sheep and goats making their rounds under the care of children, or old ladies in velvet, or sometimes just a busybody dog. Crystal is a community of about one thousand persons on the western slope of the Chuska Mountains in New Mexico. It has its own old trading post and its own relatively new chapter house, as well as a looming (and I find ugly) Mormon church.

The first time I passed through Crystal, it was from the east side of the Chuska Mountains. We had driven up Route 666 from Gallup, past miles of windblown fences along the highway, tumbleweeds and fast-food packaging plastered against the wire, gold and purple wildflowers carpeting the strip of disturbed land between the road and the fences, a kind of warfare of weed species in the trenches and an overgrazed dun-colored moonscape beyond the fence. Then we turned west (left) and headed for Washington Pass and arrived in a world that truly looked like Switzerland but was only what biologists would call Alpine. So pure! We paused, sitting off the road, and watched acorn woodpeckers ply their arena, little bullets of black and white and intense crimson, saw and listened to chickadees and nuthatches chipping and squeaking as they eked their living from the vertical world of pines they had known so long. I watched a mountain-pass stream dance like shining liquid glass past somebody's home or summer camp, a lighthearted burble of water and sunlight and shadow coiling over rock. Cliché words – verdant, emerald, coruscating – sprang to mind, and I thought that I would like to live in such a place, among the trees, the unchastened purity of the top of the world. Out past the sentinel pines – spreading east and west to arenas beyond the eye's potential – lay a pastel desert lowland, ever changing. Here, one could reasonably imagine, was what God had intended the world to be. We didn't know anyone in Crystal then, so we just drove on through.

Crystal Lake lies among the foothills west of the Chuska Mountains in New Mexico.

(Since then, it is worth noting, Washington Pass is no more. It was named for Colonel John Washington, who ran down a number of Navajos near there in 1849 – one of them being the leader Narbona. This seemed insensitive, to say the least, to a college class at Navajo Community College in the late 1980s, and they began the lengthy process of petitioning the United States Board of Geographical Names to change it. Changing the name of a geographical feature from something offensive to Indians to something honoring them had never been done. But in 1992 the board acted and it is now Narbona Pass.)

A couple of years after my first trip through Crystal, I was driven north past the grand red sandstone bastions that line the east of Route 12 out of Fort Defiance, headed again for Crystal, my brain lolling and veering, forgetting and remembering, drifting – after a few days in a Gallup hospital. How long a time I didn't know for sure. But some people had it in mind to heal me before I left the Navajo Reservation, and this takes a little explanation which will, I think, say more about the ways and byways of Navajo generosity than it will say about the electrical properties of the brain.

If some cosmic Henry Moore created Monument Valley, nobody can imagine who might have done the nearby Valley of the Gods. North and east of Monument Valley, Valley of the Gods always seems to be free of people, the great spaces between its angular and bizarre rock temples empty, a place utterly beyond comprehension even for a geologist. The first time I saw the place I was left spinning a bit. Driving onward, after several miles of reflecting on this, I pulled over on the side of the highway, confessing that I was tired. In fact, Susanne had said, "You look tired." So she took over the wheel and we headed south toward Chinle, Arizona. We were nearing Round Rock when windstorms came up on the horizon. Round Rock is where the witches evidently gather, and Susanne likes to get by it with as much dispatch as possible. At this point the sky filled with dust and, in fact, lightened. Some whirlwinds kicked up their heels on the horizon. If a whirl-wind runs into you, Susanne said, if it actually bumps into you, it makes your face crooked. That's what she had been told by some Navajo friends. So when she looked over at me and my face was contorted, my hands twist-ed like claws, she said something like "Cut it out."

The rest, as far as I am concerned, is largely hearsay.

I recall a few separate moments lying in the backseat wondering why my back hurt, and being helped out of the backseat by an Indian guy in an angelic white suit during a major dust storm. I also recall telling a doctor the date and finding it immediately funny that I was five and a half years off. A few moments in the hospital. And being in a narrow hospital bed where there was no one to give me aspirin for my back. And then being driven to Crystal.

Suffice it to say that Susanne's memories are more direct: seeing me obviously dead, seeing me eventually breathe, flagging down a trucker (with no radio), eventually flagging down a Navajo recruiting officer from Grant's (the angelic white suit – Navy) who guided her through the howling dust to the Public Service Hospital in Chinle about a hundred miles away, the doctor pronouncing me the victim of a vast and metastasizing brain cancer.

She watched me vanish into the dusty night in an ambulance, destination unknown, but in the hands of a beautiful Navajo nurse (I do recall her a bit), assuming the ambulance was headed for Gallup and catching up to it there at about midnight (Gallup is about two hours from Chinle) and finding the next day that it had been a massive seizure, like epilepsy, a sudden, violent earthquake of the brain, which, in my case, it turned out, was essentially one of a kind, with relatively minor aftershocks for several days but no recurrence since.

In the course of the four days I was in the Gallup hospital, Marie Saltclah of Crystal got wind of what had happened and visited, explaining with the gentle firmness that brooks no opposition that upon my release and before going home I was to be taken to Crystal where her family would hold a healing ceremony. This was only a year or two after we had met Marie, and while I was aware of the honor, and happy to comply, I also had no say in the matter, arriving there rather like a limp and good-natured Raggedy Andy doll.

Marie and Susanne had been introduced a couple of years earlier by a mutual friend. Having been struck by the beauty of Crystal even earlier, including a nearby lake where on lonely photographic assignments she would go for contemplation and to recharge her batteries, Susanne eventually asked a Navajo friend to introduce her to someone there. It was Marie. The two women took one look at each other and whatever it is that sets people apart vanished – millennia of separate cultures, upbringing, skin color, you name it. (I believe this can happen more often between women, but not all that frequently in any case.) In any event, before long, Marie was introducing the noticeably blond *billeganna* (white) Susanne to her sometimes astonished acquaintances as "my sister" – and this was meant in the adoptive sense, a member of the family, not in the generic way that a woman might consider all other women as sisters.

To people unfamiliar with life on an Indian reservation, people who can imagine only the vast differences between cultures, Marie is something of an anomaly – or maybe a new kind of Indian person. She seems to be thoroughly assimilated, for example, dressing in proper business clothes, including high heels, to drive to her office in Window Rock (some forty miles away), where she is an administrator of the college scholarship programs for the government of the Navajo Nation. She unhesitatingly speaks fluent English. When some Navajo students at the University of New Mexico in Albuquerque raised a ruckus about the failure of the Navajo scholarship program to take care of all of them, it was Marie who was designated to go to Albuquerque to stand before this angry group (which had gotten a lot of sympathetic, even cow-eyed, local press) and explain as diplomatically but forcefully as possible that people who were late putting in their applications for scholarship aid didn't get it. Bang. No more Indian time when you want to hook up with the dominant culture. Not everyone was delighted, but the issue did not come up again.

Marie may well be an exemplar of the new Navajo, and that makes her very much a part of the entire Navajo experience, which is nothing if not a continuing renewal. Rodger Boyd, the friend who introduced Susanne and Marie, explained this once. Navajos, he said, are like a tree that puts on a new growth ring every year. There is an essential core that never changes, but the tree must exist in and react to an outside environment, absorbing from whatever the world presents those elements that it requires to grow and persist – and rejecting others. (Of course, the rejection of many unhealthy but attractive outside blandishments is always a terrible problem, but it is not uniquely a Navajo problem.) The rings of the tree can be read: they show years of good growth and poor growth; they show scars from wounds of varying intensity which are grown over, absorbed, and buried, part of the tree's history and identity. But the tree grows on, and it is always, at its core – and in its present proliferation – the tree of its origins. There are many students of Navajo ways, especially Navajo students, who know that this is the Navajo genius.

Marie Saltclah, for all the graceful maneuvering in the Anglo world that she is capable of, remains fundamentally and obviously a traditional Navajo, participating fully in the Navajo ceremonial life – both domestic ritual and the healing ceremonies conducted by medicine men. Upon entering her house, for example, one will like as not be "cedared." She will set fire to a small pile of cedar leaves in a dish, like incense, and with a wand of eagle feathers brush the smoke onto the visitor while saying a prayer for the visitor's well-being. (When we moved into a new house in New Mexico, Marie made a point of coming, on New Year's Eve it turned out, and cedared us and the house, praying in the four directions and seeing to it that all the entrances were blessed.)

Marie knows the whole range of Navajo ceremonies. When she was younger, Marie evidently was diagnosed as having a chronic problem that could only be resolved by a Fire Ceremony, and she described to us how, at one point in this very awesome and evidently scary ceremony, the medicine man had left the hogan and returned either with, or in the form of, a bear. Such phenomena are employed, I later learned, as a kind of shock treatment in various Navajo healing ceremonies.

So when we drove into Crystal from the hospital in Gallup, I had no idea what to expect.

Marie Saltclah's house – a one-story frame building her sons and brothers-in-law built for her – lies at the northern end of the settlement at Crystal at the end of its own dirt track that turns off about a half mile beyond her family's main camp. It is in that camp that Marie's mother, Glenibah Hardy, lives, great-grandmother, matriarch, and member of the Water's Edge clan. In her eighties, Glenibah has her own hogan, where she still weaves rugs in the Crystal weaving tradition. She is surrounded by people named Clark – her daughter Irene married Jimmy Clark and they and their several sons, their wives, and their children inhabit other houses in the large clearing in the piñon woods, which also hosts a large barn that Glenibah's husband built years ago, numerous sheds and corrals for sheep and horses, and a spiffy log hogan. The daughter Irene is a noted Navajo weaver (as is *her* daughter-in-law, Margie) whose rugs have won numerous honors including the best in show at the Museum of Northern Arizona's Navajo Day. Like most of the Crystal weavers, Irene tends to muted, earthen colors – rusts, grays, rich browns – and also yellows, golds, and oranges, the colors typically

Marie Saltclah demonstrates the diagnostic use of
crystals to her daughter-in-law, Geraldine Blackgoat,
and her daughter, Waleste. Of crystals it is said, "He
can know everywhere – air, earth, water, and sun."
Below, Marie's mother, Glenibah Hardy, weaves on
a loom built by her son.

hand-dyed from local plants and lichens. But on at least one occasion Irene broke the traditional pattern at the request of a famed collector, Gloria F. Ross, who wanted a Navajo rug patterned after the horizontally striped paintings of the contemporary painter Kenneth Noland. Working from a card-sized miniature painted by Noland, Irene set out to create a rug called "Rainbow" (*Naatsiilid*), measuring 124 by 251 inches. Her husband, Jimmy, and a son had to extend her loom. Later she wrote Ross: "This rug symbolizes the strength of my family. Every strand of naturally died yarn interwoven is my family's clanship and the belonging to one another . . . the colors of the rug symbolize the array of colors depicted in the rainbow . . . the strength that protects and paves the path to beauty and harmony."

Irene evidently got a little help writing that from her son Ferlin, who had worked in the public information office of the tribal chairman and then shipped out to Cambridge, Massachusetts, to obtain a master's degree in public administration from Harvard University. When it came time for graduation, his aunt Marie took her life savings and bought airplane passage for everyone in the family to attend. In all, twenty-two people made the nearly five thousand-mile trek to and from that alien and unknown country.

This, then, was the extended family that awaited me when I arrived groggily in Crystal.

Susanne and I were quickly ushered into a huge white tepee that had been erected about a hundred yards from Marie's house. Normally, the tepee is for Native American Church ceremonies. These are ceremonies given to physical and spiritual cleansing and involve the use of peyote. There had been such a ceremony recently, and the tepee was kept up for this day's activities. Susanne and I and the family members sat on the ground in a circle, and we were introduced to a medicine man named Roy, a young man in a down vest and with what struck me as a rather fierce visage. The chief components of the ceremony were a small fire, which Roy knelt by, and a bone flute, which he played for some minutes, praying at some length in Navajo. At one point he took one of the embers from the fire, put it in his teeth, and blew on me through it. The family joined in the prayers, from time to time explaining to me what I should do. Eventually Roy told Susanne and me some private things about us that he could not have known from any source we were aware of. He identified that I had lost someone but had not properly said goodbye. Therefore, the one I had lost was still lurking there in me, creating the disharmony that had led to the seizure. With that, he blew more smoke on my back from a hot coal, took me by the shoulders, and sucked almost violently on the back of my neck, finally gagging slightly and spitting out a hunk of what looked like bloody tissue on the ground. There were more prayers and, abruptly it seemed, the ceremony was over.

Everyone reassembled in Marie's house and we were fed mightily with mutton stew and other standard Navajo dishes. There was, as I recall, a sense of gaiety, an air of fulfillment in the house. It was suggested that I pay Roy for his help – $50, which hardly seemed enough.

Doctors later were not able to say exactly what the seizure episode was, nor could they explain why it turned out to be a one-time event (very much like an earthquake with a few weeks of aftershocks). I did not, in subsequent visits, get to see Roy to ask him his views of all this, but I did get the chance to help return the favor. One night several years later, when we had moved to New Mexico, Marie called to say that we were needed in Crystal the next day. It seemed that a ceremony was under way for none other than Roy, and that I should be there to help, by way of reciprocating for his helping me. We should arrive, Marie said, by seven-thirty in the morning. So we got up at three and made the drive through the night, arriving at the appointed time in a large field in Crystal. At the near end of the field was a small house, at the far end a large shade house made of branches. In the middle was a hogan. We were ushered to the shade house, where some twenty women were preparing food in large pots over open fires. A recently skinned mutton hung from a hook, oil for fry bread sizzled, and people, some of whom we knew and some we didn't, greeted us warmly and went about their business. Huge pots of coffee simmered, and we were offered some. In due course, a number of men emerged from the distant house and gathered around the hogan, shouting what I took to be loud prayers. Some of the men entered the hogan, then came out. There was a great deal of commotion, and then it subsided. At that point, Marie told me to lead the procession from the shade house and carry one of the large coffee-pots to the house at the other end of the field. Our family was bringing food to the other family, it was explained. There ensued a feast, though Roy and some medicine men remained in the hogan. Two hours after we arrived and with my assignment completed, we were back on the road. No one told me exactly what ailment of Roy's was being healed that day, and it seemed impolite to ask, but I was honored to have done my part, however minuscule, in healing the shaman who had healed me.

Marie Saltclah's mother, Glenibah, is a healer herself of a rather specialized kind – a hand-trembler. Hand-tremblers are diagnosticians who go into what might be called a trance and divine a patient's problem, also discovering which ceremony needs to be done. Over the years Marie herself had grown increasingly aware of her own talents as a healer and, not untypically, has often brought those talents to the aid of nonNavajos. In one instance she (and her sister Irene) engaged in a long prayer session with a white friend of ours on a long-distance conference telephone call. But for long-distance effectiveness, nothing can equal what is attributed to Marie by Jim Whittaker, the mountain climber and organizer of the Peace Climb of Mount Everest as part of the Earth Day celebrations of 1992.

Whittaker's wife, Dianne Roberts, and their two sons were staying in our house in New Mexico while the climb took place, monitoring events by phone, fax, and through various diplomatic channels that stretched around the globe. It seems that when the Russian, Chinese, and American teams were nearing the summit, a great wind came up – a wind greater than anyone had ever seen on the peak; it pinned the climbers down in the penultimate camp. The wind persisted for several days, bidding fair to doom the expedition, and a desperate Whittaker got a message out by radio, asking if Susanne's Navajo friend Marie could do something to stop the wind. Marie calmly explained to us on the phone that there was nothing anyone could

do to *stop* the wind, but that perhaps it could be moved. And so Marie prayed
that day and, as Whittaker explains in his video account of the expedition,
the wind abruptly stopped, the skies cleared over Everest and stayed clear
and calm until all the climbers – in all, some twenty – reached the summit.
And when Whittaker returned, and he and his family went back to their home
in Port Townsend, Washington, they discovered that the same day the wind
had died on Mount Everest, a fierce gale had blown down a number of
giant trees at the Whittakers' house.

We members of what is called the Dominant Society tend to think of people
such as the Navajo as remote, odd, presumably affected in many ways by
our society for better or for worse, but having little or no role in the active
process of our civilization. We find many of their ways downright bizarre,
certainly not in accord with our own rationalist view of the world and how
it works. The federal agencies responsible for monitoring and predicting
the weather and fretting about the climate, for example, do *not* move winds.
It is convenient for a culture infused with scientific products, if not always
scientific reasoning, to suggest that an anecdote like that of Whittaker's
describes a number of mere coincidences. There is nothing wrong with seeking
such convenient explanations, so long as it leaves the other group – in this
case, Navajo civilization – to see the world in a way that over the millennia
has come to be convenient to them, as well as highly practical. This is called
tolerance, a virtue that is hard to come by in the best of circumstances, and
rarely practiced.

Even more rare, I think, is for people of this Dominant Culture to imagine how bizarre its ways must seem to people with a different way of seeing
things – and how much tolerance a Navajo, for example, must have to maintain anything Navajo in the face of the noisome juggernaut unleashed all
around them. Living in two such different worlds, holding each up like a
crystal and watching the light reflect from its facets without being blinded –
this cannot be an easy accommodation to make. Few Anglos do, or can.
We are an either/or culture. True or false. One or the other. Each year in
December, for example, there are news stories about people from one or
another municipality or school district (or whatever) going to court over
some public display, such as a crèche, that is tied to the religious origins of
Christmas. This is a perfectly understandable tendentiousness. But that is
not what happens in Crystal, New Mexico, where Susanne and I went one
Christmas Eve.

We went first to Marie Saltclah's house, but soon, with Marie and her
son Marcus (then a promising linebacker at one of the local schools but with
a yen to be an architect), we were standing in the unfathomable dark and
icy wind outside Irene and Jimmy Clark's house in the main camp. The
door opened, revealing a warm glow of light and heat inside. At least two
dozen members of the extended family were present, sitting in the living
room, spilling over into the kitchen. Glenibah Hardy, the great-grandmother,
sat on the outskirts near some birthday cakes with a small but intense smile
on her lips, as she listened to five girls, dressed in red, singing "Happy
Birthday" to Jesus. Behind them was a large Christmas tree bedecked with

ornaments of all kinds; a truly vast pile of presents glittered nearby. After the chorus sang various hymns, carols, and popular Christmas songs, Jimmy Clark took over. He is, among other things, a *yei-be-chei* dancer, an embodier of the Holy People, perhaps even Talking God, and with a feathered wand he solemnly went around the room, blessing each person. Then he similarly blessed the array of presents. Only then were they distributed, one at a time, with great glee and shouts of excitement. Several of Irene's sons approached and with quiet solemnity handed Susanne and me Christmas cards. And then, the presents all distributed, each person there rose in turn to say what it meant for him or her to be there.

Afterwards, there was mutton stew to be eaten, and two birthday cakes – one of which was for Marie, whose birthday is Christmas Eve. A great deal of what I thought Christmas represented had been absorbed into this Crystal family as easily as the Navajos took the Spanish sheep into their lives. The Easter before, we had been invited to attend a church service in the town of Sawmill, about thirty minutes south of Crystal. Glenibah, the eighty-year-old hand-trembler, was to be baptized into the Roman Catholic faith. To tunes so familiar as to be a physical part of our brains, we sang some old hymns translated into Navajo.

Unlike most Americans, the majority of whom have been found by sociologists to leave the church of their parents for another, or none, Glenibah and other Navajos we have met prefer not to switch but to *add* religions. Once, several members of this family visited us and, before sitting down to lunch, we all stood in a circle, holding hands, while one of the family said grace in Navajo. It lasted for about thirty minutes, and that was largely because the blessings of virtually all great religious figures of the world – Jesus, Buddha, Gandhi – were invoked for each of us. The list went on and on and finally we each took a sip from a glass of water that was passed around and dove into the feast, feeling utterly grateful and taken care of in spite of the fact that the hot dishes had grown a bit cold.

I had the sense then, and again at Christmas in Crystal, out there in the realm of the Holy People, within the history of monster-slaying, and under the protection of Changing Woman and all the other welcomed faces of the deity, that my culture – with all its divisive angels inscribed on the heads of theological pins – had plenty to learn in a place like Crystal.

Rites of Passage

We had known Melanie (not her real name) since she was a baby in a cradle board, and now she was getting married. She had sparkling dark eyes and a wondrous, mischievous smile. From the time she entered school, we had sponsored her through Futures for Children, an Albuquerque-based organization that arranges such liaisons between Indian children and people in the outside world, as well as aiding tribes in the Southwest with community development programs. In her mother's camp in Rough Rock, Arizona, one of Melanie's duties as early as age five was to tend to the daily needs of her bedridden grandmother. One summer, when she was seven years old, we brought her home with us for a visit in the tiny rural town in northern Virginia where we then lived. Her mother and she got on each other's nerves, and her mother rather hoped that Melanie would take to life in the East and do the rest of her growing up with us. That was not exactly what we had in mind, but it was not to be in any case. Melanie was fine during the days, careening around town on a bicycle with some little friends she found instantly, but with night came a deep and unassuageable homesickness. She would cling to Susanne like a lamprey, and spend much of each night in tears. After a few days, she asked us to send her home, which we did, putting her on a plane in the care of the flight attendants. She vowed calmly and firmly never to return to Virginia.

A bit more than a decade later, after we had moved to New Mexico, Melanie called to say she was pregnant and getting married in a month, and invited us not only to come to the wedding but to produce a hundred formal wedding invitations. This entailed a quick trip to Gallup, where we met Melanie and her husband-to-be so that Susanne could take a photograph of the two of them for the invitation. Melanie had lavish tastes when it came to wedding invitations, which are not typically part of a traditional Navajo wedding. She wanted Susanne to photograph the wedding itself, and she also asked Ruth Frazier, the president of Futures for Children, to come and bring with her balloons and napkins that said "Melanie and Stanley" – also atypical items, we thought. So we were not sure what to expect when we arrived on a hot summer day in Rough Rock at a little before one o'clock, when, according to the invitation, the wedding was to occur.

We were greeted warmly by Melanie's mother, her husband, and a couple of Melanie's sisters, but wondered briefly if we had perhaps come on the wrong day. Aside from the family members, the camp was empty: no wedding guests in sight. But no, the wedding was to take place in a hogan some distance up a rise from the house. The bride was dressing in the house. The balloons were whisked off to the hogan to be blown up. About three hours later, during which there was little to do but watch Melanie's kid brother practice roping with a lariat and a fencepost, people began to

Long before her puberty ceremony, a young girl receives instruction from her grandmother about the sacred nature of life and its passages.

drift into camp in pickups and cars. The groom's family arrived from Black Mesa, the huge escarpment that looms up over Rough Rock, a two-hundred-and-fifty square mile tableland that dominates the regional landscape and, on its distant southern edge, is home to the Hopi villages. This was familiar ground for Susanne – both Rough Rock and this end of Black Mesa – for it was here in the late 1960s that she had first encountered the Navajo people about whom in due course she both photographed and wrote her first book, *Song of the Earth Spirit*. We learned, as people continued to arrive, that the groom's family had pointed out that the wedding should not properly begin until the sun had reached a particular angle in the western sky – and this angle was not achieved until just before sundown.

Followed by family members, the groom entered the hogan and, walking to the left (south as with the path of the sun), sat on the floor at the far end, facing the entrance. His family sat by him to the north. Meanwhile, a small procession left the house and headed for the hogan, led by Melanie's uncle, a medicine man, carrying a cup of water. Another uncle and Melanie's mother carried food, and the bride walked among them in moccasins, deerskin leggings, a white satin skirt and blouse, bedecked in what appeared to be all the family's turquoise jewelry – bracelets, squashblossom necklaces – and a storebought white shawl with red, yellow, and blue stripes. She carried a shallow basket woven of yucca in which there was a layer of cornmeal mush. Partway along the dirt track to the hogan, Melanie's mother handed her tray of food to Susanne and told her to lead the procession into the hogan. Inside people had gathered – at least fifty – adding the warmth of their bodies to the already hot room. Except for the balloons arrayed around the walls of the hogan, it looked as traditional as could be.

Melanie sat down to the groom's right, with her family to *her* right, and placed the basket of cornmeal mush on the floor before the groom. Melanie's kin had ranged before the couple a great array of food of various kinds, accompanied by a small mountain of wedding gifts. Kneeling before the couple, the medicine man put the cup of water before them and they washed each other's hands. Then the medicine man took corn pollen from a pouch and made lines across the mush in the four cardinal directions. Speaking in Navajo all the while, he turned the basket halfway around, symbolically, I learned later, turning the couples' minds toward each other. He bade the couple to take some of the pollen and eat it. Meanwhile, Melanie's mother had interrupted once to beckon Susanne toward the ceremony to photograph it, explaining to the assembled group that Susanne was Melanie's sponsor and not just some opportunistic Anglo journalist. At another point, after the corn pollen ceremony was over, there arose a hue and cry – "Sponsor! Sponsor!" – which I discovered was directed at me. I was beckoned forward, and Melanie's mother told me to administer the "white man's vows." Now, I had not listened to the traditional wedding vows with much attention for more than a decade, but they came back more or less as I squatted down before the couple and had them hold hands. Knowing something of the Navajo feelings about death, I left out the phrase about "till death do us part," and the couple repeated the words after me, apparently to everyone's satisfaction. Then the occasion took on an air of a grand party, the bride's family passing out the feast to the groom's family, and then everyone digging in, while the presents were opened to great cries of appreciation. It was only at this point that one of Melanie's sisters made an appearance: she had been teasing her hair into a gigantic hairdo that looked for all the world like a Burmese temple. And in this cheerful mixture of tradition and modernity, tradition prevailed: both families preferred that the photographs that had been taken not be published lest people be troubled as a result – that is, witched.

Melanie's wedding was the last in a variety of what might be called rites of passage for Navajo children – some great, even momentous, others small.

Al Slinkey, who provided the drawings of Navajo motifs for this book, is a big, broad-shouldered man, who gives the impression of being handy with his fists. As a boy, he lived at the Morenci copper mine, where his father had a job as a miner. He served in the U.S. Navy in Vietnam and has held down a host of jobs on the reservation and off – from coal mining to tour guide in Canyon de Chelly. He is an artist, accustomed to the ways of white people, but highly traditional in outlook, though he has a cheerful streak of irreverence that has, in earlier times, led to a few nights here and there in jail. He explains that his grandfather got the surname Slinkey because he was especially adept at slipping into others' horse corrals and making off, undetected, with a horse of two. And when the Navajo president Petersen Zah floated the idea of officially dropping the term Navajo in favor of Dineh, Al Slinkey was among those who thought it wasn't worth the fuss and bother. "Everybody already knows us as Navajos," he said. "My grandfather told me that the word Navajo was a Taos word for thief. Well, if the moccasin fits, you'd better wear it."

Al Slinkey, a Vietnam veteran, empathetically tends the gravesite of another warrior – a nineteenth-century U. S. cavalry officer – at Fort Defiance. That the man was an enemy of his people matters less than honoring their connections.

Slink lives with his mother, who retired a few years ago as a nurse in the Indian Health Service in Fort Defiance. She and her two sisters are mad for Bingo, and go at least once a week to the Bingo parlor in Gallup, usually driven there by Slink, who finds other things to do while the ladies play. In Fort Defiance, Slink likes to hike along the high ground above the town, thinking of the old days and the battles that took place there between his people and the army. He will laugh and say, "Those old Navajos, the ones who came here to attack the fort, two thousand of them. You know, I guess they weren't real up on military strategy. They all came into this canyon from one end. No wonder they got beat."

Few of life's ironies slip past Slink unnoticed, and few of its vicissitudes have avoided his immediate neighborhood, but he is, as far as I can tell, a man who is at home in his world. What he is most proud of, one senses, is his daughter, Madonna, though perhaps now that laurel belongs to Madonna's son, Steven.

When Steven was about three months old, he laughed (as babies will) and that called for a party. The reason for this harks back to Changing Woman and her twins. When they were still infants, Salt Woman came by to visit and one of the twins laughed his first laugh. But the other twin did not laugh. Now laughter is one of the important things a baby has to do (along with crying, getting around on four "legs" and, in due course, speaking). Also laughter is one form of "language" that everyone understands. In any event, to make things right that day long ago, Salt Woman picked up the other twin and made it laugh too. Today, usually the person who makes a baby laugh its first laugh has to have a big party for all the family members.

So one day, Susanne and I were invited to Fort Defiance to join Al Slinkey's family in celebration of Steven's first laugh. It was not unlike a big family picnic outside Slink's mother's house. A relatively casual affair, it had its ceremonial aspects, too, as befits an event that was originated by Changing Woman.

Along with mountains of fried chicken, potato chips, and various kinds of salad that were piled on the outdoor table, salt had been placed in a shallow wedding basket. When it came time to eat, the people assembled filled their plates and approached Slink's daughter, Madonna, who sat holding Steven. She gave each person a bit of salt and held each plate, seeing to it that Steven also held the plate – or at least touched the food on it. Steven did not much care for this, and instead of laughing, cried piteously until all had received their plates back from him. Slink explained that the food at the party all "belongs" to the baby and, in giving it out to people, he learns to be generous, and not stingy. And until the baby laughs, his great-grandmother said, no one can give him a valuable gift, such as jewelry.

The greatest gift, it seems, comes from Changing Woman, the Holy Person also known as White Shell Woman and White Bead Woman, surely the most beloved and revered among the Holy People. She bestowed on female humans the capacities of womanhood and birth. This was during the ceremonial process called *kinaalda*. (Marie Saltclah told us that the accent is properly on the last syllable: Kee-nahl-DAH.) The word bespeaks a process that originated somewhere in the past near Gobernador Knob, and it also embodies the chief participant in that ceremony today, a girl who begins her first menstrual cycle and, therefore, receives the blessing ceremony of *kinaalda*, a public celebration of something too wonderful to overlook. The person and the process are one.

At long last, Marie's daughter, Waleste, was to become *kinaalda* and have her kinaalda. Everyone was waiting, watching. Upon the first sign of her first menses, the word went forth and the family gathered in Crystal for this remarkable moment of passage – one that used to be unheard of in my society except possibly in hushed whisperings, confusion, possibly shame and a few ignorant sniggers.

When Changing Woman gave sign that she had achieved *her* first menses, it was seen as a great and propitious occasion by First Man and First Woman. They began a four-day ceremony and celebration. She was attended by First Woman – known in this process as Ideal Woman – who assisted her daughter by adorning her with the finest jewels and beads: jet, coral, turquoise, and obsidian. The girl wore a magnificent woven dress, with moccasins and leggings. Corn of many colors was gathered, and Ideal Woman brushed and tied her hair, thus combining thought, life, and values: *hozho*. Each day of the four-day ceremony, the girl-goddess ran toward the sun, farther each day toward beauty. In the course of the ceremony Ideal Woman massaged her, from toe to head, into the strength and power of womanhood. She had, then, the capacity to bear children – the twins who would render the world safe for people. Such an event is not likely to be taken lightly in a wayward world.

Waleste's *kinaalda* was held at the camp that includes Glenibah Hardy's home and that of Waleste's aunt, Irene Clark, who took on the role of Ideal Woman. She would assist Waleste throughout the ceremony and perform many of the most important ritual tasks, embodying as she did all the physical, moral, and spiritual features of Navajo womanhood in which Waleste was to be instructed. On the first day, an off-and-on-again cloudy day in late September, the medicine man arrived and the camp was abuzz with purposeful comings and goings, long discussions of procedure, and the preparation of vast quantities of food. At dawn Waleste set off on her first ritual run – out of the camp and in a loop that took her a mile or so eastward, then back. She spent most of the rest of the day in the kitchen helping her mother and kinswomen. (The amount of food that needed preparation was astounding, and the need grew through the ceremony as more people arrived. A partial list of what was prepared and served on the third day includes dozens of melons, two muttons to be roasted, more mutton for stew meat, steaks, and a small mountain of hamburger for a meatloaf.) On the first day, a blanket was hung in the doorway of the hogan, letting the Holy People, including Changing Woman, know that a Beautyway ceremony had begun, a *kinaalda* being a kind of Beautyway ceremony.

Events made it possible for Susanne and I to arrive only on the second day, along with many others. The camp bustled, people came and went on various errands. Waleste's aunt Mary arrived – taking time off from her job as a teacher in the Crystal elementary school – and good-naturedly said to Waleste, "Well, you sure wrecked my weekend." And Waleste grinned and said, "Mine, too." Across the open area of the camp from the hogan, several men started a large fire with piñon logs, a fire that would burn till the end of the *kinaalda*. Irene Clark's son, Virgil, was put in charge of the fire, meaning, among other things, that he had to see to it that it kept burning through the nights. In Irene's house, preparations were under way for the building (there seems no other word) of a huge corn cake.

In the hogan that day, Ideal Woman dressed Waleste in the finery she would wear to the end of the ceremony, brushed her hair and tied it. An enormous pile of blankets, each donated for the occasion, was made on the floor in the westward end of the hogan, and Ideal Woman massaged the initiate from toe to head with a wooden weaving batten, all the while talking and singing to her, molding the soft flesh of childhood into the strength of a woman and adorning her with song. That night, Waleste slept in the hogan and, outside, there was thunder, lightning, and rain.

The third day the crescendo began. It started, as prescribed, with Waleste running off on a yet longer clockwise loop to the east, followed initially by a great band of relatives, including her mother and aunts who ran as far as they could and returned to camp. Later, Waleste emerged from the dawn fog on her way back to the hogan followed by several of her younger relatives and to the accompaniment of their loud cries and whoops. Throughout the kaleidoscopic events of the day there was a nearly palpable sense of ela- tion, along with a sense of the high seriousness of things. Waleste's mother, Marie, set off into the woods, led by her mother, Glenibah, to cut yucca, returning about an hour later. I was told, that having done this chore, she could no longer during the *kinaalda* cut anything, such as food, nor could she go near the fire. Just why was never explained, but I was by no means surprised that there were such taboos involved with this ceremony as in so many aspects of Navajo life.

During a quiet break, Irene's son Virgil, the firekeeper, talked about his job, cutting timber in the Chuska Mountains. He had, of course, given up the work and the money during this important event. No, he said in answer to a question, there is nothing like a *kinaalda* for boys, and he quick- ly changed the subject. His brother Fitzgerald, he said, could not work with wood – or with fire – because he once had a rash that had been cured by a Fire Ceremony. Later, Virgil drove off for a couple of hours to help some people a few miles away erect a tepee for a Native American Church cere- mony. Irene and Jimmy Clark had previously gone to a Squaw Dance at Ganado. Somewhere else, not too far away, I heard, there was a wedding. The land was alive with ceremony.

At about ten-thirty, Irene and Jimmy Clark returned to camp, having been up all night at the Ganado Squaw Dance. In the early afternoon, Marie Saltclah, Waleste's mother, told me to go over to the hogan, which I did, sitting as unobtrusively as I could on the left (or south) side of the hogan, where I had noticed men sat when present. Then I noticed that I was the only male present besides the old medicine man and his younger assistant. I also noticed that Ideal Woman was in the process of stripping the clothes off the initiate, presumably for a ritual washing, and that the ini- tiate was red as a beet. I fled as graciously as I could, returning to the kitchen in Irene's house where several women were filling what looked like a hundred paperbags with melons, boxes of crackerjack, popcorn, and candies – like Halloween favors.

As the day waned, several young men dug a pit near the fire about two feet deep, three feet wide, and four feet long. On a long table nearby women arrayed several pots of cornmeal. People gathered around in the piñon smoke and the fresh damp air and several of the women began lining the pit with dampened cornhusks laid in a clockwise direction. Then, over the cornhusks, they placed a layer of aluminum foil molded to fit the contours of the pit. Then, one after another, they poured the bowls of corn batter into the pit. All of this was done with great precision and haste, and a lady explained to me that the batter had raisins in it: if they did it right the corn cake would rise properly and the raisins would be distributed throughout, rather than sinking to the bottom. And that would bring good luck. The cake, she said, had to be buried by sundown. Waleste emerged through the crowd around the pit and, from a wedding basket, sprinkled cornmeal on the batter, from east to west. Others took cornmeal from the basket and did likewise. Then the cake was covered with more cornhusks and a layer of brown paper, the pit was filled in, the fire's gleaming embers raked over it. Rekindled with a new armload of piñon logs, the fire was left to burn through the night.

By now, it had penetrated my awareness that women make women, and this ceremony was run by women, for women, and of women. So I did not attend the all-night part of the Blessingway that began at about ten, when the medicine man announced that the singing would begin. Susanne, an honorary member of the matriarchy, did attend, and was immediately given her first duty – keeping the fire in the stove going all night. As had been done on previous days, the people in the hogan were invited to put their valuables – pocketbooks, jewelry, whatever, even Susanne's cameras – beside the pile of blankets so that they would be blessed in the course of the night. The medicine man began singing the complex songs of the Blessingway and almost all of the women, young and old, sang along. Ideal Woman massaged Waleste as before, and a woman sitting next to Susanne explained that Ideal Woman said that now Waleste was firm and strong like a woman, whereas three days ago she had been soft like a girl.

Throughout the night, individual aunts were assigned to sit next to Waleste and keep her awake during the singing. Susanne was given the four to six A.M. shift, in spite of the fact that she tends to fall asleep and awake in synchrony with the sun. From time to time, the women would loudly explain to Waleste the various duties and responsibilities of being a woman. None of this made Waleste particularly happy: she was evidently not required to attend to any of this with awe, merely to stay awake while it went on. Indeed, most of the night she tried to concentrate on her algebra homework. But at one point, someone came into the hogan and Waleste became upset. She snapped her pencil in two in anger, and the medicine man was startled enough to miss in his singing. As he backtracked and resumed the song, Waleste's mother rushed up to her and told her that nothing personal – *nothing* – should be allowed to upset her peace of mind. She had to maintain good thoughts and remain holy throughout the ceremony.

Periodically, Marie or others would leave, returning with coffee and sweet rolls during intervals in the singing, and finally the night turned to predawn. Waleste set off into the gloom followed by a band of relatives, several of whom followed her all the way on her longest run to the east and to beauty and womanhood.

And, indeed, she was a woman.

The corn cake was dug up, broken into pieces, and brought into the hogan. Everyone assembled there, and standing by her rugs, Waleste (aided by her mother and Ideal Woman) passed out a piece of corn cake and a bag of other goodies to everyone present.

And, indeed, she was a little bit more than a woman.

That morning, on the fourth day of her *kinaalda*, Waleste embodied in her own self the wonderful powers and perfection of Changing Woman. That morning, she had Changing Woman's power to heal and so she was instructed – loudly – to stand there and heal everyone in the room. As each person approached, the ladies would tell her loudly what to do. Standing behind the "patient," Waleste did as she was told: "He's too fat! Make his stomach smaller." So Waleste, patting the patient from toe to head, would concentrate a little attention on the stomach. Standing there, a mixture of shyness and power, girlhood and womanly beauty, smiling with both embarrassment and what seemed to be a delighted glow of achievement well-earned, Waleste healed everyone that morning.

Three stages of life

From the very beginning of the Navajo world, a baby's first laugh has always called for a feast. However uncomprehendingly, the baby is considered the host of the feast, thus learning generosity. This child is Steven, son of Madonna and Mike Hillis. For Steven's baby-laughing ceremony, his father, a Navy man, returned all the way from San Diego for the day.

Perhaps the most important of all Navajo ceremonies is the *kinaalda,* when a girl becomes a woman. Here Waleste Saltclah, an honor student and trombone player, prepares for her *kinaalda* by donning traditional dress and, as the ceremony gets under way, having her hair groomed with a brush made of native wild wheat. At dawn on each of the four days, she runs toward the sun.

On the first day and the last, Waleste's aunt, Irene Clark, takes the role of the legendary figure Ideal Woman, and comes to massage her from the softness of a girl to the strength and power of a woman. Family members prepare an enormous cake of corn that will be baked underground and given out by Waleste to all the guests on the last day.

Before the corn cake is buried, Waleste
(who is called *kinaalda* during these days)
sprinkles it with cornmeal.

At ceremony's end, after all the preparation of food and its sharing, the new woman has the healing power of the deity known as Changing Woman, who celebrated the first *kinaalda* at a time near the beginning of things.

With his family seated at the north side of the
hogan, and hers to the south, a bride and groom
stand at the beginning of a traditional wedding
ceremony. Once they are seated, an uncle begins
to explain the nature and duties of marriage.

An elder pours water into a wedding vase so the couple can wash their hands, symbolizing their new life. A corn cake is presented, ceremonially cut in four directions and shared – first by the couple and then by the groom's family.

When the traditional side of the wedding has been accomplished, everyone adjourns to a festive tent, where some borrowed customs are enjoyed with gusto – the sharing of a multi-layered wedding cake, the opening of gifts among appreciative *oohs* and *aahs,* the presentation of best wishes, and the simple sharing of the moment with friends and relatives.

Currents

The eastern edge of the Navajo Reservation in New Mexico is referred to as the Checkerboard Area, a mapmaker's nightmare of federal, state, private, and reservation land all interlaced and interfoliated. Agents of the Federal Bureau of Investigation based in Gallup once told Susanne and me horror stories about responding to calls in such a crazy quilt of jurisdictions – one can pass into and out of FBI jurisdiction in a matter of minutes. There are few markers that say you just left land owned by the Bureau of Land Management and are on rancher Jones's place or on the Navajo Reservation, or for that matter on Hosteen Yazzie's own private piece of property (private ownership of land is rare among Navajos but less so in the checkerboard). It calls for a great deal of understanding and trust between different law enforcement agencies, as well as property owners. The checkerboard has arisen from a convoluted series of land acquisitions and transfers almost too complex to ever be retraced, in a state not given to pristine clarity and precision in its archives of land use and ownership. Unfortunately, understanding and trust are not always the most common features of life along the borders of Indian reservations, frontiers where two worlds – and two views of the world – meet.

One such place is called on most maps El Huerfano or Huerfano Mountain, Spanish for orphaned, or defenseless. The mountain is known to virtually all Navajos as Dzilth-Na-O-Dith-Hle, which means "moving around mountain" or "changing mountain." The Spanish name is perfectly apt, for Huerfano Mountain rises out of a surrounding prairie, a lonely peak that reaches almost 7,500 feet above sea level, a sandstone and shale orphan in a vast sea of sagebrush and snakeweed. Visible for miles as one speeds along Route 44 between Cuba and Bloomfield, its craggy top hosts a tiara of broadcast antennae and around its base are the signs of natural gas development. In that sense, the orphan has been defenseless as well.

Huerfano Mountain is also about fifty miles, as the raven flies, southwest of the butte called Gobernador Knob where First Man found the turquoise figure who became Changing Woman. This is the very heart of the ancestral Dinetah. And it was on Huerfano Mountain – on Dzilth-Na-O-Dith-Hle – that Changing Woman, impregnated by the Sun, gave birth to the twins, Monster Slayer and Child Born of Water. It was here and in the arroyos and canyons around the mountain that the twins grew up, bathed, ate and prayed, and learned some of the skills they would need to rid the world of monsters and make it safe for the Navajo people. Today, in the neighborhood, there are a few distant Navajo camps, a couple of lonely schools and missions, an Indian health center, and a dirt road that leads away west to the moonscape of the Bisti Badlands miles beyond the local horizon. Not much happens here that is noticeable to people scurrying across the state,

A desert lesson: a boy gleefully mans a hose, siphoning into a cattle trough water that was previously pumped up by windmill into barrels on a pickup truck.

Sunset silhouettes the Fruitland Coal Mine,
one of many on the Navajo reservation.

but medicine men still make successful pilgrimages to the mountain –
successful in spite of the antennae – and songs of the Holyway, Protectionway,
and Blessingway ceremonies hark back to the twins and their home in this
place. It is, by analogy, a kind of Jerusalem to Gobernador Knob's Bethlehem,
its name occurring in virtually every Navajo prayer.

In 1990, a Farmington company called ICU Inc. entered into a real
estate agreement with the owner of a 160-acre plot some four miles away
from Dzilth-Na-O-Dith-Hle. The company wanted to use the site for dumping asbestos, an insulating and fireproofing material that has been linked to
cancer and respiratory ailments since the 1970s. The state environmental
department was willing to grant the company a five-year permit, providing
that any archaeological sites be fenced off and various emergency precau-
tions be taken. Archaeological surveys found little of scholarly or historic
significance. But to Navajos the planned asbestos dump was as offensive as
the idea of dumping toxic wastes in St. Peter's Basilica in Rome. The tribe
soon officially protested and the upshot was unusually favorable. The state's
environmental officer reconsidered the five-year permit, the state supreme
court threw out the company's petition that the state had no jurisdiction
over archaeological sites on private land, and, finally, the hassled company
agreed in a confidential settlement with the tribe to abandon its planned
landfill at Huerfano Mountain.

There are an estimated 77,000 Navajos living in New Mexico and
many of them are registered voters. In a state with only 1.5 million people
altogether, where turnouts are typically low, a voting bloc of Navajos has
more clout than one might expect, and while it might be hoped that the state
government was acting the role of angel in this dispute, it is silly to overlook the fact that the Navajos can make the difference in the election of a
gubernatorial candidate. But the dispute, however successfully settled from
the Navajo point of view, only highlighted a continuing problem that haunts
Indian people, the various governments (large and small) of the country,
and the American system of jurisprudence.

To put the matter as starkly as he could, Petersen Zah, president of the
Navajo Nation, took the stump in numerous forums around the country
and pointed out that American bomber pilots in the Persian Gulf wars were
ordered to avoid harming Muslim religious sites, but the same protection
is not given by the same government to the religious sites and practices of
American Indians. He objected that Indian religions, unlike others in the
United States, have to go through any sort of legal test. "Respect," Zah has

said, "should be given to a religion that does not involve going to church one day a week, but which is based on the animals, the world, and the universe, and whose church is the mountains, rivers, clouds, and sky." Such a sentiment, however unexceptionable, is difficult to reconcile with the canons of law based on private property rights and rules that do not admit the evidentiary value of oral traditions. It is a conflict that will plague even the fondest minds for a long time. In the meantime, however, the Navajos were successful in keeping a toxic landfill away from one of their many sacred places.

In the matter of uranium dumps and radioactive tailings, they have not been so successful. In 1980, the federal government acknowledged its responsibility for uranium policy in the 1940s and the resultant illnesses to workers in the mines, about a quarter of whom were Navajos, many of them now dead. It began – with glacial deliberation – to pay what might be thought of as reparations. But when the uranium boom collapsed in the 1970s, the mining companies themselves simply walked away, leaving a lot of miners out of work and the economy of places like Grants, New Mexico (a major uranium mining center on the southernmost slopes of the Navajo's sacred mountain, Mount Taylor) in an irreversible economic slump. And the deadly legacy remained throughout Navajoland in the form of 1,104 abandoned mine sites. Most of them are found in four main areas – near Cameron and Tuba City, Monument Valley, Shiprock, and Gallup. Most of the mines were underground affairs, but the tailings lie on the ground like innocent sandpiles, often studded with large blocks of uranium ore. Many are within a few hundred feet of Navajo dwellings and, quite innocently, many Navajos have used such rocks for foundations, walls, and fireplaces. Navajos, again geologically innocent, eat sheep and cattle that graze on lands and drink water contaminated by these tailings, and children play there as in a sandbox.

Complaints reached Congress from the Navajo government as early as 1983, and since 1989, Navajo officials have investigated some fifty of the more than one thousand old mines. About half have been found to be sufficiently contaminated to justify the expenditure of Superfund money – the federal government's program to clean up the nation's most imminently dangerous toxic waste sites. Only one old uranium mine in Navajoland has been cleaned up as part of the Superfund – a mine near Bluewater, New Mexico. The tribe has made a considerable effort to educate Navajos living near these innocent-looking sites of the dangers involved, but for some traditional people the idea that part of Mother Earth herself is poisonous is difficult to get across. Meanwhile, the tribe has made its needs known to Congress and promises have been made, but little action has been taken. The Environmental Protection Agency has said, on the Navajos' behalf, that "the agencies need to do a better job of communicating with each other."

One can only imagine how confusing it must seem to Navajos of any stripe, even those with some level of sophistication in the Anglo view of the world, when the government can be so laggard about one invisible cause of sickness and death that afflicts the reservation and so quick to respond to another invisible killer.

Beginning in the late spring of 1993, a handful of young and otherwise healthy Navajos were stricken with flulike symptoms that turned into respiratory problems with an extraordinary rapidity, leading to death within a few days of onset, sometimes within a mere twenty-four hours. This was, of course, what came to be known as the Four Corners illness. By the end of May, eleven people had died, public health officials suspected a rodent-borne mutation of the hanta virus that had afflicted GIs in Korea years before, the federal government had sent in epidemiologists from the Centers for Disease Control in Atlanta, the national media descended – always quick to respond to such words as epidemic and scandal – and locally at least a lot of people were calling it the Navajo flu, opening old and new wounds. Public health officials and members of the press flooded the reservation, particularly areas such as Crown Point, where a cluster of cases had occurred. Grieving family members were being asked a lot of personal questions they were unaccustomed to being asked at all, much less by alien Anglos. It is a Navajo belief that one should not mention the name of someone who has died, especially for four days after the death.

A woman collects piñon nuts from the ground – which is the proper way to do it.

At a large early-June meeting in Window Rock that was closed to nonNavajos, two medicine men discussed the outbreak, implying that the disease had struck the reservation with particular savagery (of thirteen deaths at the time of the meeting, eight were Navajos) because the people had strayed from the path of harmony. Elsewhere people suggested darkly that it probably had something to do with biological warfare materiel stored – it was claimed – at Fort Wingate east of Gallup. And some medicine men had already pointed out that it had been a particularly wet year and the piñon nut crop had been unusually great. None of these hypotheses suggested by the Navajos were taken particularly seriously by the epidemiologists, especially certain follow-up thoughts from medicine men that young people were probably not attending to the old ways and were shaking the piñon trees to get the nuts to fall off, rather than waiting to harvest them from the ground, as was proper.

Meanwhile, all the noise about the disease was having two additional effects, beyond creating dark rumors and bewilderment. One was to scare people away from the Four Corners area, causing economic losses. A major team roping event at Red Rock State Park in Gallup, for example, was hastily cancelled: the ropers were afraid to visit and perform in a place where a thirteen-year-old girl had collapsed with the disease and subsequently died, in spite of the fact that the city of Gallup had hired medicine men to render the park safe in a ceremony that combined Navajo and Christian prayers. Tourism, in fact, plummeted in the Four Corners area that season. The outbreak spread far beyond the Navajo reservation and the number of nonNavajos afflicted soon equaled that of the Navajos. Epidemiologists began to realize that deer mice were the chief carriers, and that they had experienced a population surge because of a bumper piñon nut crop, a crop where for the third time in this century, the piñons bore nuts all year round, thanks to an unusually wet season. And, happily, remedial action became possible if someone afflicted was taken immediately to a hospital such as the one at the University of New Mexico. Public health officials soon realized that it was more effective among traditional Navajos whom they visited in remote camps to talk less about such things as submicroscopic beings called viruses and to reinforce the traditional Navajo view that people and mice should be respectful of each other but should not live together. (In fact, we were told by some Navajo friends during a time when we had a small house mouse infestation that – at Navajo – this might well be a sign that we were being witched.) In due course, matters would settle down and people would go on to other concerns. Nevertheless, the pernicious idea that this was the "Navajo flu" hung on in many quarters.

In places like Farmington, New Mexico, the border town where prejudice runs high – often to the boiling point, in spite of the fact that the town's economy relies heavily on Navajo customers – there were flagrant examples of bias. Navajo customers in fast-food stores were shunned by whites. People called the hanta virus disease a "Navajo plague," and even newspapers in Phoenix persisted in calling it a Navajo disease for days after it was clear that it had nothing to do with race or culture. This was not, either, merely an ignorant redneck response – early on, when rodents had been implicated, state public health officials had asked Navajos not to perform their usual healing ceremonies lest rodent nests get stirred up in the dirt. To this, Navajo vice-president Marshall Plummer exclaimed in exasperation, "We don't hold ceremonies in barns!"

The virus and the mayhem it caused dragged on. A year later, the Center for Disease Control, needing a catchy name for this scourge, just as we need to tame such scourges as hurricanes by giving them familiar names, recommended to the proper international body that it call this one Muerto Canyon Hantavirus. Muerto means death in Spanish. This was, the CDC spokesmen said, "scientifically and culturally correct," meaning it was named for where it was discovered. The Navajo Tribal Council complained, saying that this was clearly a reference, however garbled, to a major side canyon to Canyon de Chelly called Canyon del Muerto (where Kit Carson nailed a lot of Navajos) in what is now a national monument and a major tourist attraction on Navajoland. News organizations, the council said in a unanimously agreed upon statement, had sensationalized the hanta virus as a Navajo plague, leading to discrimination against Navajos. The CDC replied innocently that it had in mind a canyon south of Grants, New Mexico, and the Tribal Council retorted that there was no such place in New Mexico, begging the CDC to alter its recommendation.

As it turns out, there is such a place as Muerto Canyon in New Mexico and it is on Navajo land – lying just within the borders of the separate Ramah Navajo Reservation south of Gallup and the Zuni Mountains. It is an obscure canyon, largely uninhabited, part of the checkerboard world of the Navajo frontiers. A case or two of the hanta virus disease occurred there, but nothing like the clustered outbreaks at Crown Point and a few other locales that caused most of the noise. The people at Ramah seem fairly well adjusted to being a colony of a colony, as it were, in the minds of the greater Navajo Nation, and were resigned to the notion that the Tribal Council didn't know their canyon existed. Still, everybody should know their geography better, and the poets at the Center for Disease Control needed work on intercultural courtesy.

In any event, the Navajo people as a whole were unduly stigmatized. In a world that is highly sensitive to epithets, it is worth noting that Navajo president Petersen Zah, in the course of addressing the students at the University of West Virginia, explained that the names of certain professional sports teams, like the Redskins and Braves, did not worry the great run of Navajos who, obviously, have a great deal more on their minds. To the contrary, that is what they are, Zah said, redskins and braves, and they are not a little proud of it.

It is a lot different to have a lethal and wholly adventitious disease organism from Korea associated with your name and reputation.

Many Navajos are aware now, more than ever, how tied they and their lives are to the vagaries of a far greater world. Had the uranium deposits in the then Belgian Congo not dried up in the forties, for example, the Navajos might not have radioactive tailings in their yards. If the United States had not needed to send troops to Korea (including, of course, the usual high proportion of Navajo braves), then Navajos might not, years later, have lost a number of tribal members to a virus that they picked up and, in addition, have been shunned by other patrons at border town Burger Kings. As secure in their own view of their world as they are, they recognize that not many others understand or care about it. As happy as they might be merely to be left alone to practice their traditional lives without any other forces impinging on them, they have long known they cannot do this. And so they seek a kind of self-reliance, of sovereignty over their own affairs that is essentially new, though once, a long time ago, they practiced both. Such a course is inevitably risky, but Navajos are great gamblers.

Economic development in what amounts to a Third World economy is a highly sophisticated kind of bootstrap operation that larger and richer nations than the Navajo Nation have struggled with for a long time. And the Navajo Nation has many, if not all, the obstacles such countries face. The problems range from demography (about half of the 220,000 Navajos on the reservation are minors); to lack of infrastructure (vast stretches without paved roads, for example); to poverty (unemployment in some areas is as high as forty-five percent, and this in a culture where a considerable fraction of the population leads a basically subsistence life largely outside the cash economy). There is a high level of many of the problems always associated with rural poverty, from ennui to alcoholism to poor health facilities and poor health. The number and quality of Indian Health Service installations is generally agreed to be low, and thanks to fast-food dietary temptations, among other things, Navajos, like many Indian populations, are subject to inordinately high rates of such related problems as hypertension and adult-onset diabetes.

At the same time, the Navajo Nation has comparatively vast resources – ranging from mineral wealth to natural beauty – as well as a huge new generation of young people who (unlike in many underdeveloped countries) have an ever-improving educational system. Thanks to cautions by the likes of Manuelito and subsequent leaders, illiteracy is essentially not a problem for this rising generation; instead, it comprises a large underutilized labor force, eager for work and eager to stay on ancestral lands. One answer is, of course, to attract outside businesses to the reservation. One notable example is the tribe's arrangement with the Holiday Inn chain that has resulted in a first-class (and badly needed) motel in Chinle along the road to the main entrance to Canyon de Chelly, certainly one of the major tourist attractions on the reservation. The motel was built largely by Navajo labor, is staffed largely by Navajos, and the overall arrangement provides training scholarships in hotel management for Navajos.

In a different vein, the U.S. Environmental Protection Agency entered into an agreement with the owners of the vast Navajo Generating Station in Page, Arizona, to reduce its sulfur dioxide emissions by ninety percent, necessitating the installation of $400 million worth of scrubber equipment. This alone will create some five hundred jobs, and others will arise from the need for housing and additional infrastructure. The tribe expects that many, if not most, of these jobs will be filled by Navajos and that, additionally, the regular supply of limestone required by the scrubbers will be provided from sources on Navajoland. This is, in a sense, a windfall: to attract other outside businesses, the Navajos helped lobby for legislation that in 1993 made all of what is popularly known as Indian Country into an enterprise zone, with federal tax incentives for businesses to relocate to reservations and hire Indians as the labor force. But more than tax incentives are needed – there must be the promise of better roads, schools, housing, and all the other amenities one associates with business zones. Banking is something that many people take as for granted as they do a local supermarket: most small towns in the United States have more automatic teller machines than the entire Navajo reservation. In terms of banking facilities, according to President Petersen Zah, the reservation is a hundred years behind the times. This is changing: in 1993, Norwest Bank of Arizona agreed to open full-service banking in Kayenta and Chinle, and improve existing facilities in Window Rock and Tuba City. Most important, this arrangement will bring desperately needed capital to the reservation to permit small businesses

A man made lake near Tuba City, Arizona.

to get a start. In all, Norwest guaranteed $60 million in loans available in the next ten years. The Navajos hope that by starting up their own retail businesses on the reservation they will be able to keep in Navajo hands the nearly $700 million of business that escapes each year into the border towns.

Developing the Navajo Nation's inherent resources is the second prong of an overall economic development drive. For example, many people still bemoan the loss of beautiful Glen Canyon, but when it was dammed to create Lake Powell, a vast aquatic recreational resource came to exist, and all the development of this resource has taken place on its northern shore. The tribal government is currently working with the National Park Service to revive an early plan: the Antelope Point Marina, which would be, in a sense, a Navajo-owned resort on the shores of Lake Powell. A road was under construction, leading in from Route 89, in 1994. In a different vein, unlike what many would say about the United States as a whole, the Navajo Nation has developed its own coherent energy policy, announcing its intention to reverse a long history of outside interests dictating and controlling Navajo gas, coal, and oil reserves. Instead, the Navajo Nation will be a full partner in any such exploitation – a position endorsed in 1992 by the secretary of energy – and to that end, plans are afoot for the creation of the Navajo Nation Oil and Gas Company. Both a development *and* marketing operation, it will, among other things, be empowered to supply the U.S. Defense Department under federal laws requiring preferential treatment for minority-owned suppliers. Eventually, the tribe hopes to sell its own fuel on the reservation at prices lower than off-reservation, thus stemming the leak of dollars into nonNavajo pockets. This would in turn encourage the creation of Navajo-owned businesses that proliferate around transportation systems. Energy price efficiency would result from the fact that a Navajo-owned energy extractor and supplier would not be subject to both state and Navajo tax – only the latter – and tax revenues would be dedicated to both infra-structure and education.

As spectacular (and speculative) as the idea of a Navajo-owned energy company may be, it pales before the potential effects of an increasingly well known U.S. Supreme Court ruling called the *Winters* Doctrine. This doctrine has to do with water and, outside of brains, there is no resource as crucial to the American Southwest (including southern California) as water. It is hard to imagine anything that has been negotiated, traded, bought, sold, agreed upon, disagreed upon, litigated, relitigated, legislated, and relegislated more than the waters that annually flow down through Colorado and Arizona and on, supposedly, into the Gulf of California – that is to say, the Colorado River system. Chasing water rights is more prevalent in the Southwest, one would happily bet, than chasing ambulances. Estimates of the amount and "ownership" of this water vary, and much of the variance has to do with one's assessment of the official flow of the Colorado as opposed to its real yearly fluctuations, but something like 110 percent of the river's water is already "owned" or at least dedicated before it even gets to the Republic of Mexico. Without the Colorado's waters, Arizonans like to say darkly, the great fruit and vegetable basket of the Imperial Valley in California would be as productive as, say, the Salton Sea. Others point out that, were it not for the Central Arizona Project, designed to ferry Colorado

River water across Arizona to the greedy lawns and golf courses of Phoenix, that sixth largest city in the United States would revert to a desert way station. On and on it goes; the exact computations are well beyond the scope of this volume. Suffice it to say that the noisy arguments in the West over such matters as mining permits and royalties or fees for grazing cattle on public lands, will almost surely sound like the squabbles in a chickenyard when the *Winters* Doctrine blows like the dust-laden spring winds, interrupting all daily life in the lands of the Southwest.

The message of this particular wind – *Winters* v. *United States*, 207 U.S. 565 (1908) – refers to the nature of treaties between the U.S. government and the tribes, when tribes ceded to the government large tracts of aboriginal lands in return for a guaranteed reservation. It doesn't make any difference, the Court said in 1908, if a particular treaty did not specifically reserve water rights to the Indians: the Indians retain water rights. This finding evidently lay relatively dormant until a dispute broke out between Arizona and California, who were squabbling as usual over the Colorado River and ran up against the problem of water rights of the various tribes along the Colorado River. The Court said in 1964 that the tribes' *Winters* rights should be based on the reservation's *practicably irrigable acreage*, adding a bit ambiguously that *that* meant a tribe has the right to "sufficient water to satisfy the purposes of the reservation." However that is computed, the point is that the tribes' rights come first, regardless of whatever arrangements have been made among local, state, and federal governments. Naturally, other water users have claimed that Indian use should be restricted to purely agricultural purposes (which isn't all that restrictive if a reservation the size of West Virginia decided to go into reservation-wide hydroponic farming). Meanwhile, Indian tribes have argued that no tribe entering a treaty willy-nilly restricted its entire future to agriculture. Why, in fact, shouldn't the Navajo decide to erect a Phoenix-type city on the banks of the San Juan River – a kind of Brasilia devoted to light industry, tourism, and the gas, oil, coal, *and water leasing* business? Both examples used here, of course, are wild exaggerations, but they serve to point out that when the Navajo do, in fact, decide to assert the extent of their aboriginal water rights, and after all the litigation, negotiation, politicking, and rethinking that will follow that assertion, the Navajo Nation – along with other local tribes – might well go beyond a kind of sovereignty. Its decisions about its share of this crucial natural resource could have profound and lasting effects on the overall economy and the daily lives of everyone dwelling in the greater Southwest of the United States.

Such initiatives and potentialities are stirring, reminding the rest of the world that a large array of stereotypical notions about Navajos – and Indian people in general – are in for some overdue revision. A Navajo energy company, out there wheeling and dealing over oil futures or whatever with the boys in Houston, seems a very far cry from the traditional view of Navajos – typified by a beautiful, broad-beamed old lady in velvet herding sheep in the lonely desert, or weaving in the silence of a remote camp tucked away in the middle of nowhere under the shadow of a mudstone mesa. But the former is a dream designed to perpetuate the reality of the latter – the complex pattern of life and belief that is personified in that old lady with her sheep.

Just how difficult the task is – to keep an eye on the needs of the marketplace *and* on the fundamentals of Navajo culture – was dramatized by an internal dispute in the early 1990s over logging in the Chuska Mountains, part of a range that runs roughly north from near Window Rock to Teec-Nos-Pos (if one includes the Lukachukais and the Carrizos). This range, a kind of backbone across the landscape, is considered by most Navajos to be essentially a male deity, just as Black Mesa to the west is taken to be a female deity. The Chuskas have been logged for ponderosa pine for a century, since 1958 by a for-profit Navajo operation called Navajo Forest Products Industry (NFPI). A major part of the NFPI operation is a lumber mill built in the town of Navajo that provides three hundred permanent jobs, and one hundred or more other Navajos are employed from time to time as loggers to keep the mill running.

In recent years, NFPI had run at a loss, facing much the same market difficulties as the timber industry elsewhere in the country, and it sought permission from the tribe to cut more trees in the Chuska Mountains than had originally been slated. A group called the Dine Citizens Against Ruining Our Environment (Dine-CARE) protested vehemently, arguing that not only would overlogging the Chuskas eventually kill the golden goose, but that the forest (one of only four on the reservation) was being despoiled to the point that its cultural and spiritual values were jeopardized. Among other things, the forest is used by medicine men collecting certain medicinal herbs that grow only at altitudes high enough to support ponderosa forests. The dispute between Navajos grew quite bitter: even Irene Clark's mild-mannered son Virgil, a contract lumberman, expressed his disappointment that a group of Navajos would want to block other Navajos from making a living. Suspicion that this was so was not diminished when, in a scenario worthy of a Tony Hillerman mystery novel, Leroy Jackson, one of the cofounders of Dine-CARE, was found dead in his car at a rest stop near Taos, according to New Mexico police the victim of a methadone overdose. Such internal disputes will surely increase as the tension grows between serving tradition and creating jobs that serve the marketplace.

A Navajo official told me once that Navajo culture was something like a ship heaving its way through the sea, subject always to new winds. In order to stay on its basic course, it has to shift, and shift again. The Navajo government, he said, is trying to develop a market-type economy not to emulate the goals – either philosophical or even economic – of the greater society, but simply to survive, to see to it that the Dine can stay together. Sheep, weaving, silversmithing these were learned from the Spanish and became part of Navajo culture. But the Navajos rejected other Spanish influences, such as Catholicism. It is an article of faith that this can happen again. The Navajo Nation is growing every day, he said, producing children, maintaining the essence of the old culture in the face of various traumas and the urge of the dominant culture over the years to "make us disappear." The continuing existence of the Navajo, he said, has been – and is – a defiant act.

Rising up like a grand galleon eleven hundred feet above a long-forgotten sea is Tse Bi Dahi, the Rock with Wings, otherwise known as Shiprock, the

Shiprock, believed to be the remains of a great bird that anciently flew the people to safety, soars above the Arizona desert, a symbol of Navajoland.

emblem of the Navajo Nation if a single emblem can be posited. To geologists, Shiprock is a classic example of a volcanic neck, the result of a huge upwelling of lava into the innards of what once was an immense mountain that itself had once thrust up from a long-gone inland sea. Just how large a mountain can be guessed by three sinuous lava dikes that radiate out from the neck into the surrounding plain for miles. The dikes were molten lava that penetrated cracks extending from the mountain's core. The volcano erupted some twelve million years ago. Since then erosion has removed almost all the mountain, leaving the soaring neck and the dikes of harder metamorphosed rock and washing the rubble of sedimentary rock down into what has become the San Juan River, into the Colorado, and thence to the sea. Geologically, Shiprock suggests a fine and enduring defiance. To the Navajo, it is the rocky remains of a once-living giant bird that materialized long ago in the Navajo past when trouble brewed, and flew the people to safety.

Each autumn, at the town of Shiprock, some ten miles northeast of its namesake, the Navajos put on a grand celebration, a country fair that is not unlike other country fairs held throughout the west. There is a rodeo, amusement park rides, booths hawking Navajo tacos, cold watermelon juice, T-shirts, and the like. But there is also pow-wow dancing, and the dignified line dancing of Navajo couples in a great circle. And there is a parade. It is an oddly silent spectacle, for the most part, with the audience lining the street outside the fairgrounds standing with what seems reverence as the parade passes. The only cheers are likely to erupt when someone on a float throws some candy into the crowd or – importantly – when a warrior of any stripe goes by, be it an Anglo tank crew, or the Henry family from Bisti whose truckbed is filled with what would seem to be four generations in uniform and a sign proclaiming that the U.S. Army and the U.S. Marines are a tradition in the Henry family. Police cars with markings from jurisdictions throughout the Four Corners area prowl past silently, along with trucks and floats representing chapters and various quasi-governmental organizations. Navajo high school bands are sprinkled among the other celebrants, batons twirling bravely, tubas oompahing to the silent appreciation. A high school combo goes by, raucously rocking on a flatbed, pausing only to cheer any sirens on the highway. And a major feature of the parade is the presence of well over fifty "princesses" who pass by during the two-and-a-half-hour event. The princesses, bedecked in traditional Navajo dresses and adorned with gleaming crowns, represent schools, chapters, and other entities, and they ride on cars that have been completely Navajo-ized, covered from stem to stern with Navajo rugs. Sometimes a princess will ride alone, bowing and waving to the crowd; sometimes she is attended by the runners-up from her local contest. They are beautiful, of course, but they have arrived at this position not in the manner of a typical American beauty contest with bathing suits, evening gowns, and a presentable hobby like singing Gilbert and Sullivan classics. These princesses are judged on their capability in such traditional women's roles as weaver, cook, potter, potential matriarch. Such a parade, such contests, are only one way of holding up something deeply Navajo in the wind that blows from all around. And as regular a feature in the parade as the princesses are signs – all variations on the theme of "Tradition, Pride, Patriotism – a Celebration."

About as far south as you can get from Shiprock and still be on Navajo land is the separate Ramah Navajo Reservation, most of which is located on a high plateau, some eight thousand feet above sea level, dominated by pinon forests that stretch over the land like a vast green blanket. Here, another, even quieter, celebration has been going on since the mid-1980s when the Ramah Navajo Weavers Association got under way, a cooperative economic and cultural venture designed to ensure the survival of the traditions surrounding sheep, and to achieve a degree of economic self-reliance in a changing world. In addition, they have undertaken experiments in organic vegetable gardening, the use of simple water catchment basins in small orchards, and other low-impact land-use schemes.

Among the early tasks of the weavers – now totaling some forty members from age twenty into the seventies – was to reestablish herds of churro sheep, working with Utah State University which had a unique program of back-breeding to produce sheep that are as close as possible to the original sheep brought here by the Spanish and eagerly adopted by Navajos. After the Navajos' defeat in the 1860s and their return from Bosque Redondo, the government instituted sheep improvement programs that rendered churros a rare – even endangered – breed. But enough of the gene pool remained here and there on the reservation to reestablish herds, and at Ramah there are several hundred of these animals now. They are long-legged, fecund, with a lamb death loss lower than normal domestic sheep in similar range conditions, thanks in part to an unusually high resistance to parasites. Occasionally, a ram has a startling four horns. Churro wool, which grows beneath an outer coat of hair, is long-stapled and low in grease and is especially prized for its lustrous sheen, its rich colors ranging from white through browns to black, and for its warmth and durability.

The association's weavers themselves hark back to the old ways – before traders encouraged local areas or chapters to develop their own particular style-signatures, and before the use of aniline dyes. At Ramah, the wool is hand-sheared, hand-spun, hand-dyed from local dye plants that are laboriously gathered from the surrounding landscape, and woven on the traditional upright looms. With all of this labor, it can take more than 350 hours to produce an average-sized weaving, from sheep-shearing to finished product. The designs may or may not be based on those the weavers learned from their mothers and grandmothers, but there is no particular Ramah style, as there is in such places as Burnt Water or Two Gray Hills. Indeed, there is a wondrous variety of individual styles. This has not helped them particularly in the marketplace, where traders are accustomed to selling styles, but the Ramah weavers persist and success is slowly coming their way. Why bother?

To stand in a shade house eating mutton stew while hanks of wool turn red or orange in great pots on open fires, while a weaver works a loom erected under a tree nearby – a quiet, matriarchal and communal hubbub of activity under an endless sky, a scene that has been repeated countless times in countless places over hundreds of years, an activity that is, however distantly, part of the greater world but carried on far from its herky-jerk clamor – to be there is to know that such a question simply does not call for an answer.

Churro sheep, now being bred back to the
original Spanish form, are the focus of the
Ramah Weaver's Cooperative, these being from
the herd of Jamie Henio, seen on the previous
pages herding his flock and weaving in his camp.
With double-horned rams, churro sheep also
have a double layer of fiber – both hair and
wool – making a much stronger wool for rugs.

Emphasis is on the traditional: here a Ramah
weaver, Lorraine Wayne, collects the leaves
of a plant called Navajo tea to make a golden-
yellow dye.

O utside her trim hogan, Lorraine warps her loom.

The wool needs to be carded into roving (previous pages) and then spun. Here, Katie Henio spins the wool for the first of two times. Taking a break, she brushes her granddaughter's hair and rehearses the songs of the girl's upcoming *kinaalda*.

In the sun of a summer afternoon, wool gathered by a group of neighbors – now carded and spun into hanks – is stirred into dye pots in a day long communal gathering. The peach-colored dye comes from madder, red from cochineal, and golden-yellow from Navajo tea.

Katie Henio looks much less benign than a kindly grandmother as she goes on winter coyote patrol while checking up on her summer home north of the Ramah reservation. At dusk she collects piñon nuts. On the following pages Katie Henio works at her loom. On the pages beyond are four Navajo rug patterns.

The following captions are for the picture gallery that opens the book:

Page 1: Brittany Blackgoat looks out at her world from her cradleboard in Crystal, New Mexico.

Pages 2-3: Afternoon sun warms the sheer rock wall of Canyon de Chelly.

Pages 4-5: The desert glows in late afternoon sunlight at Setting Hen, Utah.

Pages 6-7: A lone fisherman tries his luck on icebound Wheatfields Lake, south of Tsaile, Arizona.

Pages 8-9: Spider Rock rises from the floor of Canyon de Chelly.

Pages 10-11: A basket of dye plants and hand-dyed wool awaits use at Pine Hill, New Mexico.

Page 12: A rug from the Ramah Weavers Cooperative at Pine Hill.

Page 13: A weaver works at her loom in her camp near Monument Valley, Utah.

Pages 14-15: The enormous sky looms over Rough Rock, Arizona, near Black Mesa.

Acknowledgments

The authors have enjoyed the friendship and encouragement of many people, Navajo and otherwise, in preparing this book – too many to acknowledge properly. Foremost among these, however, have been the extended family of Glenibah Hardy at Crystal, the extended Cohoe family at Pine Hill, the Slinkeys at Fort Defiance, Jessie Cabonie and family, the peripatetic Rodger Boyd, and the staff and volunteers of Futures for Children in Albuquerque. Our editor at Harry N. Abrams, Robert Morton, has very simply been splendid.

The Navajo designs in this book were especially drawn for it by Albert Slinkey. The authors and publisher are most grateful for his contribution.